Motherhood Optional

Motherhood Optional

A PSYCHOLOGICAL JOURNEY

Phyllis O. Ziman Tobin, Ph.D.
with
Barbara Aria

JASON ARONSON INC.
Northvale, New Jersey
London

Production Editor: Elaine Lindenblatt

This book was set in 12 pt. Fairfield Light by Alpha Graphics of Pittsfield, NH, and printed and bound by Book-mart Press, Inc. of North Bergen, NJ.

Library of Congress Cataloging-in-Publication Data

Tobin, Phyllis Ziman.
  Motherhood optional : a psychological journey / Phyllis Ziman
Tobin, with Barbara Aria.
     p.   cm.
  Includes bibliographical references and index.
   ISBN 0-7657-0127-8 (alk. paper)
   1. Motherhood—Decision making.   2. Women—Psychology.   3. Choice
(Psychology)   I. Aria, Barbara.   II. Title.
HQ759.T65   1998
306.874'3—dc21   97-29367

Printed in the United States of America on acid-free paper. For information and catalog write to Jason Aronson Inc., 230 Livingston Street, Northvale, NJ 07647-1726. Or visit our website: http://www.aronson.com

With love for my parents,
Mintzi and Velvl Onheiber
of blessed memory,
whose voices echo in all that is meaningful in my life.

Contents

Acknowledgments

I wish to thank Beth Vesel for her vision for this book and for her openness and encouragement. In the evolution of this manuscript, Pamela Dorman, Stacey Weiner, and Yoel Tobin have been particularly helpful in shaping both form and content. Cindy Hyden provided the final editorial guidance with a delightful no-nonsense attitude and respect.

Barbara Aria struggled valiantly to capture my ideas and my voice. Our working hard together has been smooth because of her critical intelligence, her thoughtfulness, her sweetness, and her terrific sense of humor.

Primary gratitude, of course, goes to the women whose stories and questions are the core of this book. I am deeply indebted to my women patients, colleagues, friends, and family who generously provided me with a profound sense of the existential issues raised by the choice about motherhood.

As I was learning how to master a new word processor, I couldn't figure out how to double and triple space. I clicked too many times and received a cybermessage that I had extended the document beyond the incredibly large capacity of my new computer. The document was no longer accessible (although with technical assistance I was able to retrieve it). I feel that if I were to thank each woman to whom I am indebted I would genuinely extend the document beyond. . . . I believe that you know who you are as you read this; please know how deeply I appreciate your contributions to the meaningfulness of this book.

Achronim, achronim, chavivim: saving the dearest for last, I thank my husband, Irv, for providing the space for me to grow. His unfailing love, encouragement, and critical understanding have helped me refine my thinking throughout all the aspects of working on this book. My daughter Rebecca's very existence has blessed me with all the right questions—and even some answers.

Thank you all.

Phyllis O. Ziman Tobin

Beginnings

A few years ago I received a call from a literary agent who asked me if I would be interested in writing a book for women who are struggling to decide whether or not to become mothers. She had read a chapter I contributed to a professional book (Ziman-Tobin 1986) about the psychology of women: it was a plea to my fellow psychoanalysts to delve into the issue of motherhood with women whose clocks are ticking.

My plea was motivated by more than the desire to see patients avoid possible regret. I believe that, as women, we create our grown-up selves through the process of choosing yes or no about motherhood; this process is our rite of passage into maturity. However fraught the task of deciding may be, I want women to see this time as their opportunity to reach a deep understanding of themselves that goes beyond whether or not motherhood might suit them.

My essay was prompted by the story of a patient I had recently treated. This woman had been in psychoanalysis for many years with a well-respected practitioner who had helped her work through significant issues around relationships, her job, her attachment to her parents. In her early forties, fully analyzed, she met a man, settled down with him, and tried to start a family. She was surprised to find that, though she had conceived at the age of 26 (and aborted the pregnancy), now she was infertile. Her clock had ticked right through her analysis. She was terribly bitter about the fact that, although her analyst had helped her form a successful relationship with the man who was now her husband, he had never, during years of treatment, brought up the question that she herself, for her own dynamic reasons, had evidently been unable to bring up: Did she want to be a mother?

I feel strongly that every woman should make an active decision about motherhood before her body decides for her. Certainly, many women feel relatively at ease with the idea of becoming mothers; it feels somehow "right" to them, as it did to me. I never imagined myself without a child or children, and, having finally found Mr. Right, became a mother just five days before my forty-second birthday. But I know from my practice that there are growing numbers of women facing the dilemma of our times—women who, at the age of thirty-something, find themselves stuck between the fear of "now" and the fear of "never." Either way there's a risk. The question is, will you take that risk with eyes open, or with eyes closed?

This is a book for today's women. It is a book for women with options—which, unfortunately, in our time still means primarily well-educated middle-class women; an individual's culture is integrated into her psychology, and therefore into her notion of choice. It is a question of what is expected of you and what real possibilities you experience as yours. Never before have we been faced with such a range of options, and not only because of the availability of reliable birth control, legal abortion, and reproductive techniques. As women, we have laid claim to our bodies and to the right to shape our destinies. We have begun to redefine *woman*. We are even redefining *mother*.

Who would have thought, just twenty years ago, that so many single women would one day choose to have babies all alone or that just as many would be able to define themselves as whole and happy without being mothers? That large numbers of women would be opting to continue in high-powered careers *and* be mothers—to have it all? Who could have imagined that lesbian couples would one day parent adopted children or have their own biological families; that women of 50 or over might choose to become pregnant; that women with fertility problems would be thinking about having their own biological children? Even today these are not easy options. But they are real ones.

And because we have options we must think about them.

This does not mean that women have to come to this decision alone; typically, the decision about parenthood is made within the context of a couple. But because I believe that today the choice of motherhood is ultimately a woman's choice—even for the woman whose impulse for or against parenthood is at variance with her partner's—this book focuses on the internal conflicts that make it so hard for some women to know what *they* want.

As a psychologist, I have worked with many patients conflicted about the issue of motherhood. One of my jobs is to help women search deeply into themselves and figure out which decision is the right one for them. I am not claiming to provide the answers. But I can help women explore certain important and psychologically meaningful questions about themselves and help them to find a personal point of balance.

I am not saying that ambivalence will vanish or that there will be no regrets; nevertheless, a woman who makes a conscious decision based on self-knowledge can accept whatever negative feelings she may have and move along with her life. The more fully we accept responsibility for our choices, the less our regrets turn into bitterness.

Most important of all, in helping women make their choices I have learned how the task of choosing can be transformed from something overwhelming into a systematic process that encourages not only constructive decision making but personal growth too.

This book describes that process: one of bringing into awareness the unconscious parts of ourselves that are typically buried and at the core of women's conflicts around motherhood. By bringing to light the unconscious underpinnings of fears and fantasies, I hope I can free the conflicted woman from feelings of not knowing or being afraid to know what she wants, open up her real range of options, and set her on the path toward discovering the best choice for herself as well as a clearer sense of who she is and wants to be. I know from my work that, however conflicted you are, if you can struggle through this process of self-discovery you will end up feeling more comfortable both with the life you have created for yourself—as a mother or a woman without children—and with yourself, the mature woman responsible for having created such a life.

One of the driving forces behind my book is my desire to cut through certain assumptions about what is "natural" for a woman to want and do—a desire whose full significance I realized only when I first met with the agent who suggested I write this. The magic moment came over lunch when I said, "You know, if I were to write this book I would have to say that the idea of maternal 'instinct' is not at all helpful."

The agent raised an eyebrow.

"The idea that it's in a woman's nature to want to have babies is a lie," I went on, half expecting her to interrupt with the kind of angry argument I had so often encountered. "The woman who chooses not to use her biologically given capacity for motherhood is no less normal, no less feminine, no less natural, no less grown-up, and no more selfish than the woman who feels a real urge to mother a child."

To my surprise the agent looked extremely pleased and said, "Do you know how many women want to hear that?"

It marked the turning point for me. As it came together in my mind, I realized all at once that any woman struggling to make a real, rational choice about motherhood has to feel equally free to choose "no" as to choose "yes." How can she attain this freedom if she accepts the stigmatization that inevitably goes with the choice not to mother?

I believe my position makes both psychological and political sense. As a psychologist, my whole life's work (as well as this book) is predicated on choice and change. There is nothing inevitable about motherhood, even if women have been mothering for centuries, even if girls have always thought of themselves as mothers-in-the-making, even if most women are gratified mothers who love their children very much. You can be or not be. You can ignore the social pressures that make you feel you must; you can overcome the personal anxieties that make you feel you can't.

No doubt any independent, consciousness-raised woman of the late twentieth century will be thinking: "Of course I'm free to choose!"

It's not so simple. Lingering beneath the surface of our fully developed conscious minds are subliminal "voices"—residues from our experiences in the worlds we've inhabited since birth—that confuse our thinking and make us less rational, less free, than we imagine ourselves to be. These voices whisper about the things we "ought" to feel and want; they create conflicts in what we think we *do* feel and want. Most difficult of all, they make us secretly ashamed and fearful of the part of us that hesitates to jump automatically into motherhood—so secretly that we might not even be aware of it ourselves.

To choose freely we have to make these voices audible. One of my tasks in writing this book—as in my practice—is to help women learn how to listen, and then how to quiet the voices that sound most false.

Every woman's issues are unique, of course; every woman comes to the decision about motherhood with her own chorus of voices. And every woman has learned her own way of dealing with the big turning points in her life. But in my experience of working with women who are struggling to choose about motherhood, I have found a certain universality in the factors that underlie conflicts around this choice. And I believe that there is a particular kind of psychological journey that can lead not only to an answer, but to a pinnacle in our self-development as women.

It is not an easy journey. And as it begins, it may be hard to imagine finding a path through the dense tangle of feelings that the thought "Do I want to be a mother?" can inspire.

1

∞

Choosing: The Rite of Passage

Why do I believe that the process of consciously and deliberately choosing about motherhood is so important today in any woman's life? Rational choices are always the best ones, of course, but my point goes beyond that. I believe that when we engage ourselves wholeheartedly in the process of consciously deciding whether or not to be mothers, we define ourselves in the most important way a woman can. And that process of self-definition is what ultimately brings us to maturity.

I believe that choosing—whatever the answer ultimately is—is *the* rite of passage for a woman today. Rather than celebrating maturity as the daughter shaping herself in the image of her mother, this rite of passage is about a woman's coming to terms with herself as distinct and separate from her mother. It is each woman's way of creating her grown-up self, each woman's journey of self-development, whatever the ultimate decision. It is her avenue to self-discovery.

SOMEDAY IS NOW: THE EMOTIONAL UPHEAVAL

As Adrienne Rich (1976) wrote, to choose about motherhood is to enter a realm of "decision, struggle, surprise, excitement, and conscious intelligence" (p. 280). The surprise, and the struggle, begin at the moment when a woman first realizes that her journey has begun.

Most of us grow up expecting that we will do it all, never imagining that motherhood is something we'll have to think about. It will simply happen someday—after college, after graduate school, after getting two feet firmly planted in a career, after a few years of freedom, after cementing a marriage. "Someday" is always somewhere far off in the future.

It can be awe-inspiring to realize that suddenly "someday" is *now*. It can feel as if just thinking about it might change you forever.

You don't have to be ambivalent about becoming a mother to experience this upheaval. Women who always assumed they would become mothers in due course, but who never gave it much thought, may experience it when they reach a certain point in their lives that kindles the spark of "now?" It might be, "All my friends are having babies—it must be time"; it could be sparked by family pressure, by a partner who wants to start a family, by an impending promotion that would mean an all-consuming commitment to career, by an unintended pregnancy.

At the moment of reckoning, there is a feeling of "Wow! Is this really me? Am I really thinking about being a parent? Who me? I still feel like a kid!" Mixed in with the excitement are often feelings that range from mild anxiety to turmoil and panic—feelings that, when they find expression, tend to fall under the rubric of "Am I ready?" It is a question that can be both useful and misleading.

Am I Ready to Grow Up? To Choose?

What does "Am I ready" mean? Many women ask themselves this question as they find themselves on the brink of the decision, and generally what they are thinking is, "Am I ready to have a baby?"

Instead, I encourage women to ask themselves, "Am I ready to choose?"

After all, what does "grown-up" signify to a woman who has lived independently, who may be married, who has a job that may involve heavy responsibilities? Isn't she already a grown-up person?

When a woman asks herself if she is ready to grow up, she might be thinking, "Am I ready to take on the responsibility of being a mother? Am I grown-up enough to have a child of my own?" Our mothers and fathers were the quintessential grown-ups in our lives—and *they were parents*.

But how true is this motherhood–adulthood equation?

Certainly it was true for previous generations of women. There was no other model for mature womanhood. Only by becoming a wife and having a baby could my mother be recognized as having joined the society of adult women that her mother was a part of.

My grandmother was considered an adult at the age of fourteen when she married and had children, even though she and her new family continued to live under the same roof as her parents, as members of an extended family. It was the fact of the daughter becoming a mother like her own that defined her as grown up.

The equation no longer holds. It is not becoming a mother that makes you a grown-up; it is choosing yes or no and thereby defining yourself as a separate individual. We can no longer become fully adult women simply by taking on our mothers' roles or living their experiences—or by rejecting those roles and experiences out of fear. Far from it. As contemporary women, we expect to forge our own kinds of adulthoods. And to varying degrees we have been expected to by our society, even if not by our immediate families. We have been encouraged to develop ourselves in such a way as to give ourselves increasing options.

Conversely, choosing from among our options helps us to develop ourselves as mature individuals. It forces us to ask ourselves certain questions about who we are and what we want to be. In order to make your own grown-up decision, it must be one that is not governed by who you always thought you would be, who your mother wants you to be, who your culture expects you to be. It means seeing yourself as objectively as possible. In other words, it means finding your mature self. You can look very grown-up on the outside—married perhaps, successful in your career—but still be your girlish self if you have not grappled with this task.

Am I Ready to Choose?

Being ready to choose implies a readiness to take on the responsibility for making the best decision, and an autonomous one. It means being prepared to define yourself by asking yourself questions like:

"Who am I?"
"Who do I want to be?"
"How do I want to live my life as a woman?" and also,
"What makes me a woman?"

It means being ready to really experience yourself as a separate individual whose choices are not governed by—although they may end up replicating—what is expected of you or what has been deemed "natural" for you as a woman.

It is a very grown-up thing to do.

Whether a woman decides to take on the responsibility of mothering a child or not to, she becomes responsible for herself and her own destiny. As Simone de Beauvoir emphasized almost half a century ago, we are each of us responsible for creating our own life's narrative; this is what gives meaning to our being, and what renders us subjects rather than objects. In our struggles to be autonomous individuals, we make ourselves who we are through the decisions to which we commit ourselves.

And the decision about motherhood is the most momentous of all. Through it we define ourselves irrevocably and in the most universal of terms.

It is a wonderful thing about this moment in history: you can choose a course that makes sense for you and find a place in the world where that choice is acceptable. At the same time, choice often brings with it a certain amount of anguish—or at least very hard work. So, I believe, do all meaningful decisions; no big deal.

CHOOSING AS A RITE OF PASSAGE: DISCOVERING YOUR GROWN-UP SELF

In many traditional cultures the passage to adulthood is envisaged as a bridge that leads from an incomplete, embryonic state to a complete, adult state; the rite of passage itself represents the journey across the bridge. There is no way to adulthood except by crossing this bridge—a journey known to be supremely difficult. The intense emotional and physical experiences required of the initiate symbolize the fact that on your journey you must leave behind your childhood self, and all that self depended on, to be reborn as your adult self. It is a metamorphosis of the inner person.

Although we have no rituals to define it, the rite of passage of a woman choosing about motherhood is no less difficult. It too requires that she redefine herself and her relationships with important people in her life and, in a sense, become a new person—her own, adult person who is not dependent for her sense of self on her identifications with her parents or the identity created for her by society.

At the least, this process can bring the same kind of tension that any journey toward maturity can bring, magnified because of the enormity of this decision. There is a feeling of apprehension about leaving behind the familiar self, a feeling of "I'll never be the same again." In more difficult cases the separation a woman must make from the self created through her childhood and from her old notions of what her life is to be can bring real anguish. Either way, out of her journey is born the woman who is complete as a person without children, or the woman who will mother a child.

Separation: Losing the Old Self

Every major transition in life can be heralded by feelings of anxiety in varying degrees: "Am I ready to give up who I was or might have been and become someone new—even slightly different?" Many of us experienced these feelings when we were about to leave home and go to college, when we applied for our first serious job or were on the brink of marriage. The process of becoming a woman who has chosen is no exception.

As with all those other transitions that mark our movement toward autonomy and adulthood, making this choice means changing the patterns of our lives. It means redefining the nature of our bonds with parents and other significant people. We become different in the way we see ourselves, and we are required to make adjustments in the way we function.

It is a process that has its own tension, much like the tension experienced by the 2-year-old who runs away from mother to play in the sand with the other kids, then runs back to sit in her lap. As much as we want to grow, as much as we want to take the next step in our development as women, we find ourselves clinging to the safety of the familiar and of who we are. So the excitement of growth and newness is mixed with an underlying fear. Am I grown-up enough to make this decision? *Do I want to be so grown-up?*

The idea of losing the self you have known for so long is sad and scary. Like the adolescent who, while fighting for independence, clings to those pieces of herself that are linked with childhood, the woman who is faced with the task of defining herself as an adult fears that she must mourn the loss of her girlish self— the irresponsible one, the one who likes to party, the one for whom all roads are still open.

"I'll Never Be the Same Again"

Kathy's Story

It was precisely this change and loss implicit in choice that frightened Kathy. She had assumed she would have her first child a couple of years after getting married because it was what her mother and both her sisters had done. The fact that, unlike them, she did not marry until she was in her early thirties and well established in her private practice as a pediatrician did not alter her assumption. Once she and her husband were settled in a home of their own, she expected that parenthood would follow fairly promptly.

It was not until shortly before her second wedding anniversary that Kathy realized the time had come. She panicked. If she stopped taking the pill, as she had planned, there would be no turning back, no way to recapture the life she was now leading. Suddenly she had to make a choice between what had seemed a natural step in any woman's life and the path she had followed so far. Everything about the way she had imagined her life proceeding, so seamlessly, so automatically, was turned on its head.

Kathy knew she didn't like changes in her life. She hated to move, even from a cramped apartment to a more spacious one, and didn't care much for redecorating. She had pursued a constant course in her profession. She had never jumped from boy-friend to boyfriend in her youth as most of her friends had done, and in fact had married the third man she had had a relationship with, expecting the marriage to last forever. Change felt too dis-tracting to her. Even *thinking* about having a child felt distract-ing. People she knew who had taken the plunge were always tell-ing her, "You'll never be the same again. Life will never be the same again." She knew it was true. She had watched friends become mothers and slip into a different world.

Then again, it was an experience she did not want to miss.

I assured her that even were she to decide against being a mother, her life would change—and so would she. I encouraged Kathy to look at all the aspects of her life and contemplate whether they would feel different to her were she to decide against motherhood. As she began to explore how she and her husband would feel without chil-dren, how she would feel among her peers, what her job would mean to her, she began to see that the meaning of it all would be quite different once she could no longer live with the illusion that all roads were open to her: whether or not she decided to have a baby, she would never be the same again. Ultimately Kathy decided that she would have a child, although she would not start trying for another year so that her choice could be separated in her mind from the echoes of her mother's and sisters' choice.

Separation: Finding an Adult Identity

A friend of mine once told me that her 12-year-old daughter had recently said to her, "You know, I'm so much like you, it's awful."

"And what did you say to that?" I asked my friend.

"I told her, 'I'm the only model you've had. But as you go along you'll decide what parts work for you and what parts don't. You'll digest what you like and throw out what you don't. That's what growing up is all about.'" I was impressed by how open my friend was to her daughter's development as a separate individual; she did not want her to be a clone of herself.

Typically, our first world is our life with our mothers. Because we are dependent upon them and therefore see them as all-powerful, their word is *the* word; the messages they send are internalized as truth. For some time it is our only truth. That is why—especially for women whose mothers for one reason or another did not give them the latitude to try out different ways of being (as my friend seemed able to give her daughter)—finding a separate adult identity can be a real struggle. And because engaging in this struggle can feel like a threat to the attachments we form with our mothers, some women are too afraid even to begin. I have treated women who, though they appear to be perfectly mature individuals, cannot start this journey of separation without a great deal of work and professional help.

Netty's Story

Take a patient of mine, Netty. Netty first came to me when she was 37. She appeared very mature on the outside. I remember her walking into my office looking perfectly elegant in her simple black dress with matching pumps and purse, her blond hair combed into a chic French braid. Netty projected a sense of having her life all together. She had been taking care of herself for many years and she had a busy social life and a steady job as a librarian in a fancy private school. She had had the same boyfriend for seven years.

Netty came to me depressed. Her boyfriend was a married man. She hated her job. And far from feeling like a grown-up on the inside, she felt very childlike. She did not have the husband, child, or house she believed all grown-up women should have. In ways that she hated, she saw herself as completely overshadowed by her giant of a mother—a "real" grown-up whose image of adult womanhood she had tried to emulate, right down to the lipstick color, and now knew she was struggling with in her adult life.

Even though she consciously disliked the kind of person her mother was, unconsciously she struggled with the problem of identification. If she tried to be unlike her mother, then how was she to be a woman? Without her mother's trappings of womanhood, she could never feel as if she had made it into the club. But she could never have those trappings because she was not good enough. The way she saw it, she was a "have-not" and always would be.

Netty was stuck. My job as her psychoanalyst was to help her move forward in her development by helping her to find her own way of being a woman.

I vividly recall one session where she was working on her relationship with her mother—not the person she had come to know as an adult but the mother of her childhood. Netty told me about a day when she was very little. Her mother had taken her shopping for shoes. They went into a department store, where Netty caught sight of the shoes of her dreams—"gold, diamonds and rubies and big bows." She pointed them out to her mother, who made no attempt to conceal her horror.

"No!" she exclaimed, as if Netty had wet her pants. Netty felt completely humiliated at having chosen the "wrong" shoes to like.

Netty's mother wanted her to have a pair of shoes that would make her look classy, not the shoes that would have made Netty feel like the pretty little girl of her dreams. She could not accept Netty for who she was—a 5-year-old with perfectly age-appropriate taste. Her self-absorption prevented her from tuning in to her daughter. She was harsh in her intolerance of Netty's differentness, and Netty, who needed her mother's approval, carried the harsh voice with her. She was always afraid of being "wrong" and therefore humiliated. How could she become her own kind of woman, with a separate identity, when she was constantly afraid of being a source of displeasure to her mother?

Netty's inner experience of herself was one of constant worry that she was a failure. She assumed that everyone, like her mother, had everything. She was to be a paralyzed have-not because she could never look as naturally "classy" as her mother, never find a man as good as her mother's, never have as successful a life—including motherhood. Even in her thirties she was constantly measuring herself up against the image of womanhood set by her overbearing mother.

During another session, Netty heard some coins jingling in my pocket and said, "Oh! You have foreign money on you!"

She assumed that I must be a "have" of such magnitude that even the coins in my pocket must be exotic.

I, wishing to show the difference between what she felt I had that she could not have and what in fact I did have, quickly picked the most banal explanation I could think of for the few pennies I was carrying: "No, "I told her, "this is change from dog food I just bought in the supermarket."

Netty laughed. She got the point. She had assumed I had what she felt she could not have, mirroring her experience of her mother. It was a turning point in our work.

I spent several years helping Netty create a view of herself as a woman separate from and different from her mother. This meant her becoming more conscious of her conflicted identifications so that she could become more independent in her views, values, and desires. As she began to see that mom had actually needed her daughter to be a pale version of herself, Netty was able to struggle toward an image of what a grown-up woman could be that did not depend on her mother's definition. She discovered, for instance, that she actually preferred herself with loose, unlacquered hair, her face without makeup. In fact, Netty finally discovered that she did not really want to be like her mother in either looks or person. But she still wanted that grown-up woman package.

And then, in her mid-forties, Netty met Mr. Right and, to her surprise, became pregnant. Here was her chance to have something she had always assumed she wanted but could not have. It was probably her last chance. But did she really want this? Would motherhood be the right choice for her at this moment in her new relationship? Or ever?

Jeff, her new boyfriend, did not want a child at this time. He had older children from a previous marriage. Nevertheless, he said he would be supportive of whatever decision Netty chose to make. After all, it was her body. But he would not be a parent to this child were Netty to choose to have the baby.

In order to make her choice, Netty would have to mobilize that new sense of herself she had gained by working so hard in therapy. In weighing what this man meant to her against her feelings about motherhood, she expressed her fear that, as much as she had grown to be her own self, as a mother she could still be different enough from her mother. Also, she said, she was not sure that she had the courage or strength to be a single parent. This was not the have-not Netty speaking: it was a woman who had an objective view of herself.

Netty decided to have an abortion. She came to my office to review her reasons and as she left we both had tears in our eyes. Yet we both knew that she had made a decision that was hers alone. It felt like the right thing for her to do. Her new relationship was a priority; she really felt fulfilled by it.

Six months later, Netty and Jeff decided to marry. Shortly before the wedding, she came to see me and noticed a photograph of my daughter tucked away rather obscurely, I thought, in the corner of a bookshelf.

"We have to talk about babies," she said.

Netty went on to tell me that she had recently taken care of a friend's little girl whom she loved dearly. She had enjoyed their time together, but Jeff had been jealous. Rather than resenting his need for her singular attention, she seemed very happy to have him as the focus of her life. She also told me that she had been struck of late by the fact that she rarely had moments when she longed for a child of her own. In glimpsing the photograph of my daughter, she realized that for the first time she was not envious.

Netty felt complete, satisfied—even without children. She was now a "have," not a "have-not." After a long and painful journey—her rite of passage—she had finally defined herself as an adult woman who, unlike her mother and regardless of what her mother wished, would live a full life without children.

In the process, Netty also decided to change her career: she had been a librarian working with children, and was now undertaking further education in library sciences in order to get a job in a college research library. Having accepted her new sense of herself, she was free to reorient her life.

2

Opposing Pulls

CHOOSING: THE JOURNEY

The process through which I have helped conflicted women find a place where they can feel comfortable enough slowing the pendulum sufficiently to decide "yes" or "no" is a complicated journey of self-exploration. Reaching this place involves teasing out, in stages, the various strands or "voices" that make up the conflict. Although many women are able to undertake this journey alone, good psychotherapy can certainly help. To a large extent, success depends on asking the right questions.

Along the journey, women generally find they are able to rescue themselves from the flood of undefined emotions that overwhelmed them when they realized a choice had to be made. They can discover the reasons they both want and do not want to become mothers, and by weighing the pluses and the minuses understand how, whatever the choice, that choice makes the most sense for them as individuals.

One Woman's Journey

Introducing Jean

Jean, a 34-year-old art dealer who was used to making split-second, million-dollar decisions on the auction floor, came into my office terrified by the idea of becoming a mother—and terrified by her terror.

During our first sessions she kept saying, "What's wrong with me? Am I crazy?"

I told her that the only thing wrong with her was that she thought she was crazy because she was conflicted. I pointed out that there were very good reasons why she felt so torn and that we would have to figure out what they were. She would not be stuck, I told her, if there were not something in her history that brought her to this moment not knowing which way to go.

Jean told me she had always assumed she would have a baby; it had just been a matter of waiting for the right time. Up until now, her husband and she had been living on one income—not enough, she felt, to support a family.

Jean's husband, Mel, was a painter who occasionally did back-drops for a theater company and once in a while sold a painting for a pittance. Far from resenting this, Jean had been perfectly content being the breadwinner, a truly modern woman. In fact, when Mel told her he was going to look for a "real, grown-up" job as a graphic artist, she wasn't sure how much she was going to like it.

Then Mel got a wonderful job. Jean took him out to dinner to celebrate, and as they were sitting in the restaurant he said, with a big grin on his face, "Everything's ready now. We can think about starting a family."

"I was furious with him!" Jean told me. She had screamed at him not to put pressure on her; now, of course, she realized he had not been trying to pressure her at all. *She* was the one who had been saying, "One day, when things are right."

"That's when I realized, something's going on. My reaction scared me. I felt like a big baby and I really didn't understand why."

Something *was* going on. Jean recalled having snapped just a few weeks earlier at a good friend when she interpreted the friend's waxing rhapsodic about motherhood as deliberate pressure. In fact, the pressure was internal. Somewhere inside, Jean had known for a while that the time was now; she just hadn't let herself become aware of it because there was something so scary about the prospect of having a baby.

Since that evening at dinner with her husband, Jean had spent endless hours thinking about babies until her ambivalence had become an obsession. Every little thing made her think about the subject: seeing a woman pushing a stroller, walking past a school yard, and, most of all, hearing yet another friend tell her, "Guess what! I'm pregnant!" Completely stuck, she had tried to surprise herself with an answer—a quick, "Yes, I'll just do it." But as soon as she faced it head on, the other side slammed on the brakes— "No! Not so fast!"

The thought of going ahead and having a baby terrified her; the thought of never having one terrified her. It was at this point that Jean brought herself into my office for a consultation.

TEASING OUT THE STRANDS OF CONFLICT: THE STAGES OF THE JOURNEY

Any question so deeply personal and significant as whether or not to become a mother is bound to be woven from many strands. The process of making an active choice involves teasing out these various components and looking at them individually.

In working with women who are exploring their conflicts, as well as with those who wish to understand their choices more profoundly, I have found that the strands nearly always coalesce around three core areas:

- Fear of change and the loss of control change brings
- Worries about being "normal"
- Issues around the meaning of "mother"

Each of these areas is explored in depth in the following three chapters. Here I want to give an overview of the journey and look at how Jean arrived at the choice she felt was best for her.

As I helped to make Jean comfortable enough to begin on her journey, I encouraged her to start by expressing anxieties at the uppermost level of her consciousness—aspects of her life and feelings that were most available—and to work gradually deeper, uncovering voices that were more and more hidden from her consciousness. This process, common to all psychoanalytic therapy, is like peeling away the layers of an onion. It is the best way to get to the core issues. Human functioning being what it is, we have many layers of protective insulation that have to be peeled away before we can reach the source of our conflicts.

Stage One: Fear of Change

Most women come to the decision about motherhood with some very real worries about tangible things. These vary, but might include money, time, career, relationships with partners, getting fat. These are the issues women generally struggle with as they swing back and forth on the pendulum: I want to, but how will we afford it; I want to, but I'm up for a promotion and don't know if I really want to give that up. There might be one or many such anxieties, but underlying them I generally find a far less tangible fear of change.

Sure enough, when I first asked Jean how she understood the fact that she was so stuck, she told me that she was afraid her career would suffer because if she had a baby she knew she would not be able to leave it with a nanny.

"What would leaving it with a nanny mean to you?" I asked. I wanted to help her uncover whatever shame she felt about not raising a child 100 percent by herself.

"Why have a baby if I can't take care of it?" she answered. She quickly went on to tell me that she was afraid of how much so many things in her life would change. Worst of all, she did not know how or how much, or if she was either ready or willing for it to change. "I don't know if I'm able to take that risk," she said. "In fact, I don't know if I'll *ever* be ready."

I suggested to Jean that she be as concrete as possible and describe all the things she thought might happen. What followed was a tangle of anxieties: She loved her work and how it made her feel; would she be able to work as much? Their standard of living could plummet and if it did and they had to count pennies and stop doing some of the things they enjoyed doing, everything might suddenly start feeling very grim; would her relationship with her husband change? She pointed out that they had made a point of keeping things equal, and that might change with a baby *and* his new job. "I'm so used to being my own person, even in my marriage," she told me. "I'm really only responsible for myself and the cat."

There were other anxieties too. They lived in a wonderful apartment—Jean's before their marriage—and she had always felt at home there. "I've grown up so much in it. And I know we'll have to give it up because it's not big enough for us and a child." She had no idea what they would be able to afford now; they might even have to leave the neighborhood.

Somewhat sheepishly, Jean told me that was worried about what would happen to her body. She was scared, she said, of getting fat. She knew her body was sure to change and, as she said, she had worked very hard to keep her figure. "It's very important to me because I was chubby as a kid, and I'm always afraid I'm going to be chubby again, so I have a trainer, I work out twice a week, I watch my diet." What if she never got back into shape after pregnancy?

Many women experience anxieties about their bodies when they imagine becoming pregnant. These might include worries about succeeding in getting pregnant; nurturing another life internally; the sexual body being overtaken by the lactating, nurturant body.

I wanted Jean to realize that all of her anxieties added up to a fear of losing control over a life that she had designed to be a perfect fit. So I pointed out that these were the things she was sure of—her job, how to take care of her body and maintain her optimum weight, her apartment, the nature of her relationship with Mel (although she was already worried about how that might change with his new job).

"And now you're thinking about taking a tank of who-knows-what and ramming right into that citadel." I assured her that it was not unreasonable to worry about change and regaining control. Hanging on to what we know is tried and true, even though the pull toward experiencing what being a mother might be like is significant—that's why there is a conflict. We really have no idea about how it is going to feel or what is going to happen, and the problem is that *there really is no way of knowing*. Jean knew that many things would change in her life were she to choose motherhood, and it was not something she could have any control over.

The way to make change less scary is to explore the fears. Quite often, if we can spell out what we are afraid of it becomes less frightening, because an unspecified fear is scarier.

I asked Jean to look at her worst fears and consider how likely, how inevitable, the pitfalls really were.

Jean's worst fear—scarier than moving to a new neighborhood or losing her footing in her career—was losing control over her body. I wanted to explore with her why this was so frightening so that she might be more able to control how she dealt with the anxiety, if not the outcome.

To that end, I asked Jean what losing control of what her body looked like would mean to her.

"I don't want to look dumpy like my mother."

What did looking like her mother mean to Jean?

In looking at what frightened her, Jean opened herself up to something she already knew (without knowing she knew it): that her anxieties about change, though very real, obscured more complicated and less conscious issues. In order to continue unraveling the strands to find out why these issues carried so much weight in her mind, we had to look deeper.

LOOKING DEEPER: LISTENING TO INNER VOICES

Looking deeper means listening to the subliminal voices that are typically at the heart of our conflicts around motherhood. One of the reasons there is so much conflict is because of the weight of societal and familial messages or voices about women as mothers—fantasies, images, and myths—that lie buried in our unconscious. They become part of our thinking and feeling, so enmeshed in how we view ourselves and the world that we think they are our own—fixed parts of ourselves that are immutable and beyond question. These voices become a part of our conflicts, particularly as they play against the earliest voices that we as individual women have received during our own, personal histories as daughters.

Messages about motherhood have always existed. Women have always had mothers as models, and society has often defined how women will use, or not use, their biological capacities to bear and nurture children. But in the world of the contemporary woman—and particularly for the woman who has internalized some of the feminist values of the past twenty years, or whose mother's experience was shaped by such voices—the messages are often at odds with one another.

In the process of making the unconscious conscious, I find it helpful to think of those competing and often paralyzing inner voices or influences as a chorus, a chorus that is sometimes harmonious but, in the case of a conflicted woman, mostly disharmonious. As long as the chorus is simply a noise in our heads we cannot really listen. In order to tease out our inner conflicts it is necessary to separate from the cacophony the discreet melodies that have been internalized over a lifetime, the way good stereo speakers separate the sound of the violin from the sound of the piano.

The point is to make each individual voice of the chorus audible. It takes a fine psychological tuning of the ear.

By making audible each of our inner voices and distinguishing between them, we can identify the different pulls acting on us—the "shoulds" and "oughts" that are the cause of our conflicts. By analyzing them and where they come from, we become more objective and need no longer be ashamed of the parts of us that say "no." And we can choose to listen or not to listen. Which voice is more meaningful to my own sense of myself as the woman I've become? Which voices no longer make sense with the passage of time? Which voices ring most true?

Stage Two: Cultural Voices

The most accessible of our inner voices are those whose source is cultural—the ones that shape our unexamined assumptions about what women should be, do, and feel. It was in the hope of uncovering those voices that I asked Jean what it would mean to her never to have a child. I wanted her to really explore how she might envision life without motherhood, and for that possibility to be a legitimate option in our work together. As I pointed out to her, she had a wonderful job, a wonderful marriage; what would be so bad about not adding a child to all of this?

"I don't know," was Jean's answer. "Something would feel terribly wrong but I can't grasp it." As she continued, it became clear that even entertaining the thought of never having a child felt somehow wrong to Jean. It scared her to think that in ten or twenty years she might still be childless. "Something tells me it's not a real option," she said.

What voice was that telling Jean she should not even consider remaining childless? What voice made the word *childless* so bad?

Although on an intellectual level Jean, like so many women of her generation, rejected the traditional linking of women with children, on an unconscious level it was nevertheless very compelling.

Our cultural voices fall into two groups: first, those voices that sing an age-old song about women as natural mothers and nurturers, and second, more contemporary voices that address issues of personhood. Although these voices conflict with one another, ultimately they are all talking about the same thing. They are talking about what it means to be a "normal" woman.

In my work with Jean I tried to help her sort out these voices, become conscious of them, and redefine normal for herself as a feeling of being comfortable in her own skin. She knew that, because of the way she had been raised, being successful in the world was important to her feeling at peace with herself. As we talked, looking at experiences in her life that made her feel "whole," it became clear that there was also something about her experiences with children that felt very right.

"I just always saw myself as being a mother like my mother was," Jean said. "For me, that's a big part of what being normal is."

Stage Three: Mother's Voice

Our personal sense of normal is influenced to varying degrees by our perceptions of our mother, depending on how like or unlike her we feel ourselves to be, or feel we ought to be. Even though we might choose to live our lives very differently from the way she lived hers, she is still our earliest model for what a woman is.

This leads to the third and paramount area: mother's voice. In working with conflicted women, I help them to look very carefully at what "mother" means to them, what images the idea of motherhood conjures up, what anxieties it inspires. This voice is the hardest of all to hear clearly because it is one that we internalize from our earliest, preverbal days. Making it audible is a matter of recapturing how we experienced our mothers—both the early mother of our childhood *and* the woman we came to know later as a person in her own right. This might not be so easy: a mother who was ashamed of her feelings about motherhood and tried to mask them may have emitted an unclear message. And for a woman whose mother was ambivalent, unhappy, unloving, or self-absorbed, this may be a particularly muffled voice.

Jean was well aware that the history of mothering in her family was fraught with distress. Both her grandmother and her mother had suffered terribly from postpartum depression; her grandmother had been hospitalized as suicidal, her mother had been terribly depressed during her children's early years. Jean knew the facts. She did not know how they impinged on her own feelings about becoming a mother.

As we looked at Jean's mother's history, she asked me: "Do you really think that has anything to do with the way I feel now?"

I assured her that it did, and wondered why she should doubt it.

"Well, it was so long ago! It was a different life, a different time."

There may be things we know about our history. And it may be only in the therapeutic process that these facts come together in terms of our understanding of ourselves, our expectations, our fears. It is certainly the most efficient way. Jean needed help in understanding that she was worried about repeating her family's history of maternal depression. She was quite justified in this worry; she clearly was vulnerable genetically to postpartum depression.

We talked some more about Jean's mother.

"I never had any doubt that she loved us," Jean told me, "but she made it clear to us that she had sacrificed a lot by staying home to care for us, especially when we were little." In Jean's memory her mother had been much more comfortable when she returned to work as a teacher, around the time Jean's little brother started grade school. When Betty Friedan's *The Feminine Mystique* was published in 1963, Jean's mother knew it was about her.

Would nurturing a child feel as uncomfortable for Jean as it had for her mother? Would she miss being able to put all her time and energy into her work?

It was Jean's father, a successful architect, who had in many important ways been the more intuitively nurturant parent; the one who played games with the kids and read them their bedtime stories. In many ways it was Jean's identification with her father that created her most positive pulls toward motherhood—the "spiritual" side, as she put it, some special contact she could make with children that she had first experienced as a teenage babysitter. In talking with children and telling them stories, Jean felt she could broaden their understanding of their world. She could excite them as well as comfort them, just as her father had done during her own childhood. And *that* felt very gratifying.

WEIGHING AND BALANCING

It is my experience that for most women conflicted about motherhood, one life event tips the balance. Sometimes it comes out of left field and has nothing to do with any of the original pluses or minuses: somebody close becomes ill or dies, making the idea of creating a new life seem very positive; family moves away, creating a yearning for a family of one's own creation; difficulties develop in the relationship with a partner and suddenly the idea of raising a child together feels all wrong.

Whatever the decisive factor, it is very often emotionally based. And that's okay. A perfectly good final choice can have everything to do with "it feels right" or "it feels wrong" as long as you have listened, through a rational process of self-inquiry, to all the voices that contribute to that feeling.

The way we imagine ourselves as mothers—whether we imagine it feeling wrong or feeling right—is influenced not only by our experiences of being mothered and by the images of motherhood with which our culture provides us, but also by images we have retained of ourselves in the mothering role. It could be one illuminating moment from the past, an ongoing experience such as having enjoyed or not enjoyed babysitting as a teenager, or even recent experiences with the children of friends or family. Accessing this kind of information from our memory can help us clarify for ourselves which of our voices are most consonant with who we are.

In the course of our sessions together, Jean would often tell me about a close friend of hers who had become a mother some months earlier. After the friend had become pregnant, Jean had been very worried that the two of them would drift apart—after all, their experiences would soon be so divergent. So Jean's friend had suggested that they adopt a pattern of regular weekly visits together. In agreeing to do so, Jean also chose to visit as a way of possibly desensitizing herself, through exposure, to her fear of motherhood.

Largely as a result of these visits, Jean gradually created a clearer picture for herself of what motherhood could mean in her own life—not the motherhood her mother had experienced, which she had been so frightened of repeating, but something of her own making that came out of her own history as a woman separate from her mother.

Jean told me that she had been developing a special relationship with her friend's baby as he grew. "When I arrive now," she
said, "he crawls to meet me. It feels terrific." In fact, she said, the
more time she spent with him, the more she felt as though she
wanted a baby of her own. All her reasons for not wanting to have
a baby were still there. But her desire for motherhood had begun
to feel more powerful. "It's just like falling in love," she said. "It's
an emotional thing."

Jean's feeling of connectedness with her friend's child was the
same feeling she remembered from her teenage years, when she
had felt that special kind of relationship with the children for
whom she babysat. The sense of gratification she had received
from this experience had always been her primary, if intangible,
pull toward motherhood. Now, as she reexperienced it, it became
more tangible and tipped the balance for her.

MOVING ON WITH AMBIVALENCE

Once a woman has come to respect that her conflict makes sense,
she can accept that whatever her choice—to be or not to be
a mother—she is likely to experience moments of regret. The
ambivalence she feels now will not disappear altogether. But if
the choice has been her own, based on an awareness of who she
is as an autonomous adult, the regret will not be filled with bitterness. It is the choices we make passively, without being conscious
or in control of the influences at work, that we are likely to end
up regretting most bitterly—as if the choice had been imposed
from the outside or "just happened."

Even after she had made a choice to become a mother, Jean
could not completely shake off her fear of repeating her mother's
and grandmother's history of depression. She knew that she could
medicate the biological aspects of postnatal depression if she had

to. But she wanted to make sure her "psychology" was different enough. The work of the therapy was to emphasize the differences that made her her own person and not a clone of her mother.

Jean was quite aware that her mother's depression lifted perceptibly when she resumed work. Why, Jean mused, had her mother waited so long? Jean, watching her friend manage mothering and a high-powered career, could gradually see that *her* life would not have to stop if she had a baby. She would not be repeating her mother's life in this very significant area.

Also, Jean was able to accept that she would always be an ambivalent person. She would have to live with that.

Sure enough, several months later, when Jean finally suspected she was pregnant and went for a test, she told me that as she had waited for the result she worried, "What if I'm not pregnant?"— and then the next moment, "What if I *am* pregnant?"

She was.

3

The Fear of Losing Control

$\mathcal{M}$any of my patients have been women confronting the question of motherhood in their early- to mid-thirties. Already in control of much of their lives, they worry, "How will motherhood affect all of this?" It is a fear that, I believe, underlies all the initial "what ifs" so many women express when they come face to face with the possibility of becoming mothers—fears that fall under the rubric, "What if my life changes or doesn't keep moving along the way I'd hoped?"

This chapter is for the woman who believes she wants to be a mother but is stopped in her tracks by those "what ifs," by the fear of change and the unknown, and, on the deepest level, by the fear of losing control over a life she has worked very hard to put under her control. It *is* scary. But, as I hope to show, there is a way of coming to accept with less trepidation the possibility of yielding to the unknown.

Exploring these fears is an important first step in any conflicted woman's journey: first, to be able to put the fears aside and move on to deeper issues, but also because while we are afraid of change, we cannot make a truly free choice. To a large extent, the choice about motherhood *is* a choice about change. Choice reflects control, but change implies some loss of control. For a woman to stay in control of her life by choosing thoughtfully about motherhood, she has to be open to the notion of losing some control, even over those aspects of her life that she wants least to change.

THE FEAR OF CHANGE

A Well-Designed Life

Diana was in her late thirties when she came to see me about the debilitating panic attacks she had been experiencing for some time. An editor for a major fashion magazine, she was in a long-term live-in relationship with a successful photographer, Bruce. The two of them had shaped a life for themselves that both found very satisfying. Although they were each busy with their careers, they also led very active social and cultural lives. They were a glamorous couple; they went to the theater, explored restaurants, saw movies as soon as they came out, attended openings, dined and partied with movers and shakers. In fact, their presence at social functions was both a requisite and a perk of each of their jobs.

Diana's Story

Diana's had not been a straight or simple path. She had started out as a model during college, done very well, then chosen to give up modeling because she was sick of the way being "managed" felt like being herded. Hesitantly, she redirected herself into the magazine world with the confidence that, if she took the right steps, worked at it hard enough, and used her wits, she could be successful. And she was.

Diana's history with relationships had been more troubled. She had been involved with a series of men, first in several exploitative relationships during her model years, then with nicer men, before her involvement with Bruce.

The panic attacks that had brought her into therapy had actually become less frequent over the years; she consulted me because each attack stood out in sharp contrast to her improved life. As we began to work on her panic disorder through both psychotherapy and medication, she began to feel better.

Diana's life seemed all mapped out now except for one thing: as far as I could tell, she had never dealt with whether or not she wanted to have children. It wasn't even that she had been thinking "one day"; it seemed to me that she was a postponer in the extreme.

Since I feel that, as a therapist, my job is to encourage women to explore the question of motherhood before the clock stops ticking, I brought up the issue with Diana. I did not want her to wake up one morning in her late forties thinking, "My God, it's too late!" I also expected that her avoidance of the question pointed to some issues that needed to be uncovered in therapy.

One day, when Diana was talking about her age, I asked her: "What are your thoughts about motherhood?"

She dismissed my question with a harsh: "I have none." She paused, then looked at me scornfully and said, "This must be your agenda—it's not mine."

Sensing in the intensity of her reaction a fear of even thinking about the idea, I told her that whether or not I had an agenda, I felt it was important for *her* to make an informed decision.

"You want me to have a baby," she said.

"No, I want you to think, I want you to have some thoughts, I want you to make an active choice. Either way is fine with me."

But Diana would not discuss it. And that was that.

I knew Diana was convinced on the surface that she did not want to be a mother. But she was projecting onto me her desire to be one. This is "splitting" the ambivalence. Instead of experiencing uncomfortable mixed feelings, a person consciously feels one way unequivocally, but meanwhile puts the opposing feelings in someone else's heart.

Women conflicted about motherhood often split their ambivalence with their partners—"*I* want to, but *he* doesn't." Diana's partner wanted a baby in a "someday" way that she did not experience as pressure one way or the other. She split her ambivalence with me. I was the "yes" to motherhood; she was the "no."

Over the next few weeks, whenever I brought up the subject of motherhood—if only to rule it out—Diana would roll her eyes and respond with, "Oh, come on!"

I wanted Diana to realize that before we could begin to talk about her conflicts, she had to understand that she really was frightened of the issue of motherhood, and we had to understand why her fear made sense. And I also had to convince her that I personally did not care whether or not she became a mother.

I asked her why, though she insisted that it was I who wanted her to have a baby, she was not able to articulate why motherhood was not for her. I assured her that there were good reasons for her not wanting to become a mother, but until she explored them she could not make an active choice.

Slowly she began to believe that I really was neutral, and moreover might be onto something important for her.

One day she said, "Well, we only have to look at my mother to know why raising kids is the last thing I'd want to do."

Diana had told me about how bitter her mother had been. "She couldn't stop telling me what a hard life it is. If that's what motherhood means, why would I want it?"

A difficult, self-absorbed person, Diana's mother had been abandoned by her husband for a younger woman when Diana was 4, and had never gotten over it. In her experience her life was ruined because here she was, saddled with a daughter to raise by herself. She made it clear that, although she loved Diana, her very existence contributed to her misery.

What if Diana's relationship with Bruce were to change and spin out of control—maybe even *because* of a baby? Things were bound to change. What if they were miserable with their lives as parents? What if she didn't like Bruce as a father? What if she really lost her figure and Bruce got turned off by her body, or Bruce stopped liking her? Diana knew she was very much like her mother. "I'm not easy to be with either. Sometimes I can be very demanding and unsympathetic," she would tell me.

Diana could not deal with the risk of being left holding the baby all alone as her mother had been. And the only way she could control that eventuality, regardless of whether the marriage lasted, was by not having a baby.

The Need to Stay in Control

Control over one's life is a normal human need: The infant's attempts to master tasks like self feeding are all geared to gaining some kind of control; taking care of oneself is the first step toward taking control of one's destiny.

Diana, like many women who have created reasonably successful lives for themselves, was particularly frightened by the prospect of losing control. As I pointed out to her, even her initial response when I had suggested that she make a considered choice about motherhood had been, essentially, "Don't control me—it's your idea, not mine." That same fear had permeated her life from a young age.

I wanted Diana to understand how natural it was for her, as a person with her particular story, to be so fearful. So I reminded her of a story she had told me: as a teenager she had been at a party where someone had spiked her drink. She had never forgotten the horror of finding herself terribly out of control.

Diana had also, for as long as she could remember, lived in fear of vomiting, which for her represented losing control over her body. This fear was in the back of her mind whenever she thought about herself pregnant and possibly experiencing morning sickness. She could not bear the thought.

I assured her that, yes, she might lose control. She might vomit, she might find herself leading a very different life. But she could be in control of her *choice*.

No one can predict what will happen in your life if you add to it such an unpredictable element as a baby. Your relationships, your body, the way you lead your life, your sense of yourself all have to adapt to new circumstances. It is simply a question of when and how you will resume control.

To a lesser extent, nobody can predict what will happen if you choose to be childless.

SEPARATING THE ISSUES

It is not unusual, when we feel conflicted about something that is going to affect our lives in so many ways, to create an overarching theme for our cluster of related, yet ultimately separate worries. After all, change in one area of our lives does create change in other areas. But we cannot challenge our assumptions about how bad those changes would be while we continue to see them as one generalized blur.

By asking herself questions about each separate area of her life, a woman enables herself to explore more fully all of her very real anxieties. Instead of simply worrying about losing control, she can think about what might actually happen if she lets go of the control she feels she has over her life.

What would it mean to you to count pennies? Why are you so afraid of having to move? Why does the risk of a change in your relationship scare you so much?

In exploring these questions she can get to some understanding of why specific fears feel so scary. Perhaps she's afraid that her marriage will turn into her parents' marriage. How realistic is that fear?

Having looked at each issue separately she can more easily identify and explore what is most weighty for her and gain a greater understanding of herself. This is important. We cannot control or predict what might happen in our lives. But the more aware we are of ourselves and the more we understand our own complexity, the more we can distinguish between what we can control and what we cannot—and the more gracious and easy on ourselves we can be about the things that are beyond our control.

Of course, a good sense of humor about life's ironies certainly helps!

Worries about Career

Worries about career are powerful ones for many women in the throes of deciding about babies. "Do I want the struggle of balancing a career and mothering? Can I manage it? Do I want to try to have it all, with all the headaches that can entail?"

You might ask yourself, "Will I lose interest in my job?"

"Will I still be able to move ahead in my career? How will I feel about myself if I'm not?

"Will work still be satisfying to me if I don't give it as much of myself as I have in the past?

"If I take a break from work, will I get rusty?

"What if I never want to go back to work after the baby?"

Some women wonder whether they will feel comfortable leaving a child in someone else's care, even if they know, intellectually, that children thrive with good mother substitutes and they themselves thrive in their job. It's a question of how you define *mother*, of how important your work is to your identity as a person, of how much effort you want to put into exploring those conflicting voices within you.

In the face of all the uncertain rewards and uncertain losses of parenthood, and faced with the unknown you of the future, the integrity that your life has achieved over the years begins to dissolve. Until now you thought you knew what you wanted, where you were going, who you were. No longer. When it comes down to it, it's a question of, "Do I want to experience this thing that everyone says is the ultimate experience for a woman? Or is it an experience I can and should do without?" After all, contrary to the myths that permeate our thinking, motherhood is not every woman's most positive experience.

Worries about the Changing Body

A woman who has controlled her weight and her fertility just as she has controlled her life in order to "become" something can be terrified by the idea of letting go. She worries about how her body will function and how it will respond to pregnancy. In a sense, her body becomes a metaphor for her life: If she loses control over one, will she lose control over the other?

In her book *The Mother Puzzle*, Judith Schwartz (1993) points out that many women control their weight in order to retain an "androgynous" form that corresponds to and affirms their "androgynous" selves: "A slim form suggests an ability to manage, a trait admired in business. Whereas excess weight implies emotionalism and lack of control, traits that are condemned" (p. 153).

Fear of Getting Fat

Our culture's emphasis on thinness has become so insistent, it contributes to emotional turmoil in huge numbers of women thinking about pregnancy—not just those with eating disorders.

Many a woman who has dieted, worked out, jogged, or otherwise tried hard to keep in shape finds herself looking at pregnant women and at women who are mothers with a keen eye. She asks herself questions that cannot be answered about things more or less beyond her control: How big will I get? Will my legs swell? Will I be left with stretch marks or cesarean scars? Can I tolerate that kind of assault on my sense of physical self—even the temporary distortion of pregnancy itself?

When a woman expresses these kind of fears in my office, I generally ask why she thinks such changes in her body, dramatic though they may be, would be irreversible—especially for someone who evidently knows how to care for her physical self.

We tend to think that because some things will change forever if we become mothers, the same is true for our bodies. But in the case of our bodies, "forever" is just a state of mind, one that might be reinforced by hearing our mothers say, "I never could get my figure back after the babies."

The fact is, our mothers did not work at being slim the way women do today. During our mothers' times a matronly figure was not considered as unfashionable as it is today, and neither was extreme thinness considered healthy. Mothers looked at their daughters—today's conflicted women—and worried that they were becoming dangerously scrawny. We in turn looked at our mothers' fuller figures and decided we *never* wanted to look like that—like mothers. We understood this disregard for slimness as coming with the maternal role. Caring for your child meant letting go of yourself, which was fine for *them*: mothers weren't supposed to look sexy anyway.

Fears about Sexuality

Which brings me to the next point.

Ever since the pill became the birth control method of choice, beginning in the '60s, women have been able to choose to be sexual without having to worry about babies. Sexuality has become disconnected from procreation. With this disconnectedness, sex has taken on a different meaning for women: its goal is self-fulfillment, which brings us into greater equality with men who have traditionally seen sex this way. My mother used to warn me, "A man puts on a clean shirt and leaves. A woman is never the same again. There's no such thing as sexual equality." Today, a woman can put on a clean shirt and leave too.

We have learned that in one sense the sexual body is ours to do with what we like—we control it. But what happens when we think about getting pregnant and reconnect sex with procreation? How will we feel about our breasts, as part of our sexual body, when they are transformed into things to satisfy a hungry baby?

If there is a chance that we might have a problem conceiving on demand, our feelings about our sexuality may be laden with guilt. It is not unusual for a woman to worry that any prior sexual experiences, any abortions, any use of birth control, might have compromised her ability to get pregnant—should she decide to. She might wonder, even, if she will be "punished" for all the other things she did to her body in the past—perhaps the smoking, the drinking. . . . She might suddenly see her body as impure, not a place where a baby can grow.

Fear of Infertility

These thoughts lead to the fear: "What if I don't get pregnant?" The woman who has had total control over her fertility, in the sense that she could be almost 100 percent sure she would not conceive, now faces the fact that, however fastidiously she charts her cycles and gauges her times of ovulation, she cannot really control when or if she will get pregnant. If it doesn't happen right away, does it mean she's infertile?

What would it mean to have a body that isn't functioning normally?

As contemporary women we value ourselves as equals of men. But we also want to experience ourselves as feminine. So the fear of infertility—of having no choice, of being less than a woman— can be as powerful as the fear of getting pregnant.

If it *does* happen right away, am I ready? Is my body wholesome enough?

The very notion of pregnancy triggered all these anxieties in Diana, and more. There was nothing she could do to guarantee a pregnancy free of morning sickness. What she *could* do was try to control her fear of nausea in the same way that she had learned to control her panic attacks. Here at least was something within her control—something, like her panic attacks, she could deal with more actively. She could choose to work on this in the interests of making pregnancy less frightening, or she could make a reasoned choice not to get pregnant.

Worries about Relationships

One of the hardest factors for a woman to ignore in considering motherhood is her relationship with her partner. Certain vague anxieties come up repeatedly. If you were to define and elaborate on them, they might resemble the following questions:

Will my partner really share the burden of parenting? If he doesn't, how will I feel about him? If he does, will I feel comfortable about sharing the maternal role?

How will my partner respond to being a parent?

How will our sexuality be affected?

Will we fall into stereotypical male/female roles if we have a baby? How would that feel?

Will the relationship survive the stresses of parenthood? If not, how would it feel to be a single mother?

If I take time off for the baby and end up earning less, will I still feel like an equal partner in the relationship? Would I feel a loss of power? Would my partner still respect me? Or do I expect to be supported? Is that a realistic thing to expect?

Both men and women change in themselves and in their relationships to each other as they make the transition to parenthood.

This need not be frightening. The question I suggest that patients ask themselves is, "What is there in the relationship that I'm worried will change?"

One of my patients, when she explored more specifically her fears about having a baby, discovered that she was scared it would upset the sense of a partnership between equals that was so important to her and her husband. Although they would surely share the burdens of parenting a child in theory, she knew all too well that in practice the woman tends to be the one who is most tied, most responsible, most willing even, to give up some of her own life for her child's.

I encouraged my patient to ask herself what this would mean for her were it to happen. How would it affect their relationship? Would she risk losing earning power? If she did, would she feel terribly dependent? Was it a feeling she was afraid she would hate because her self-esteem was rooted in her ability to be financially self-sufficient? Or was she secure enough in herself and her equal standing with her husband to be able to accept some financial support from him for a while without feeling disempowered? Was she willing to risk it?

The risk was clear for Diana. Her relationship with Bruce could spin out of control and she would be left to raise a child alone, just as her mother had done. Ironically, it was after we had been working on her motherhood fears for a while, and she and Bruce had finally married with the intention of at least thinking seriously about having a baby, that the whole relationship question started to trouble her so much that she swung right back to, "No, I can't."

Diana had dealt successfully with her panic attacks. The idea of vomiting no longer terrified her. And we had been working on other issues that had a bearing on her decision about motherhood. But soon after her marriage to Bruce, he lost several important photographic clients and it looked as if his time in the limelight was over.

This was a real problem for Diana. She could no longer respect him; sometimes she wondered if she even liked him. She found herself snapping at him, demeaning him, treating him the way she had treated other men in her failed relationships. She was afraid that she was losing the ability to be sympathetic and in her anxiety was becoming more and more demanding, like her mother.

Parenthood, she feared, would only compromise the relationship more. Even now, they tended to get tangled up in issues of power and control within the marriage, such as who made more money, who was going to take the dog for a walk. That would only get worse. The only time things were good between them was when they were sharing what they both loved—the parties, the theater, the dinners. That would change if they were to become parents.

How *could* she have a baby?

ASKING DEEPER QUESTIONS

In general, if any specific concern feels particularly weighty to a woman, she needs to ask herself why she is someone for whom this is so important. Why, although a part of her wants very much to have a child, does the problem of her career weigh so heavily? Why is she so afraid of what parenthood might do to her marriage? Why is the thought so troublesome that her marriage might replicate her parents' marriage? The point is to make the sources of the anxiety as concrete as possible.

Women can ask themselves questions: How realistic is this? How likely is it that my partner might become who my father was, or that I, in my relationship with my partner, might become who my mother was in her relationship with my father? Is this something within my control?

Fear of Replication

Asking questions such as these allows a woman not only to achieve a more realistic sense of how much control she could or could not have in this area of her life but to free herself from assumptions that she might not even know she is making—most important of all, the assumption that she is fated to replicate her mother's life, step by step.

The first step in the replication is having a baby; that in itself is an assumption. We are not fated to repeat our mothers' journeys *to* motherhood any more than we are fated to repeat the steps of those journeys *through* motherhood. But if a woman avoids taking that first step simply because she is afraid that subsequent ones will inevitably follow her mother's path, she has not looked clearly enough at why having or not having a baby makes sense for her. It's a matter of looking at your current life and the resources at your disposal, internal and external, for coping with the changes parenthood will entail.

Diana was perfectly aware that her overarching fear was of replicating her mother's experience in some inevitable way if she too became a mother. She would drive Bruce away as she believed her mother had done to her father; then she would lead a miserable life as a divorced woman with a child to raise and support alone.

She sensed something automatic about the way she was with Bruce since their marriage. Although she could work on this in therapy to gain more control over her response to Bruce, she still had no guarantees that the relationship would last. But she could ask herself: "If the marriage ends, will my life necessarily be the same as my mother's was?" She could look at her mother's circumstances—her mother as an individual, her mother's time in history, her mother's feelings about working hard at a job—and see the extent to which her own circumstances, her own self, her time in history, and her feelings about her job were different.

There were also questions Diana could ask herself about the recent turn in her feelings toward Bruce. She wanted the marriage to be egalitarian, she said. Did she also, on some level, want to be taken care of as her mother had not been? To what extent did she look to Bruce to be a father to her because she had had no father? How much did that feed her resentment of his professional reversal, which frightened her so much?

Weighing and Balancing

Diana and I were working on some of these questions, and she and Bruce were working on their relationship in couples therapy, when something happened out of the blue that made Diana's pendulum swinging come to an abrupt halt and caused her to decide "yes" unequivocally. Ironically, it was something that blew Diana's control issue sky high and raised the odds on single motherhood enormously. Bruce was diagnosed with prostate cancer. With surgery and chemotherapy he might live. But he might not.

Suddenly, in the face of Bruce's illness, the idea of having a baby seemed to both of them very life affirming and symbolized for Diana her love for him—a love that resurged when she thought she might lose him.

Although she was still somewhat afraid of being left holding the baby, because of the work we had been doing in treatment Diana was able in these circumstances to distance herself from the fear and make her decision. After three years in therapy, her self-knowledge was such that she knew why she felt the way she did, what her fears were based on, and the extent to which her nightmare of living out her mother's life was likely to come true. She could hold in her mind two related yet separate thoughts: that her life *felt* as if it was heading the same way as her mother's, and that if she had to, she hoped to be able to cope with her husband's death differently than her mother had coped with abandonment.

All this shifted the balance for Diana, even though she was no less afraid of taking the risks that had been scaring her so much. She decided to have a baby.

MOVING ON WITH AMBIVALENCE

Essentially, the questions addressed in this stage of a woman's journey amount to: "Given who I am and the life I am living, do I want to add a child to it? Can I accept the changes parenthood brings? If I'm afraid that my life would spin out of control were I to have a child, is that fear realistic? Is it a risk I think is worth taking, or not?"

If, after considering these questions, she is still telling herself, "I think I want to have a child but I'm worried my career will suffer," she might in fact be feeling, "I really think career is a priority for me, but I don't feel comfortable with the idea that I might not want to be a mother." Or she might be feeling, "I really want to be a mother but something about the idea—something I can't quite define—troubles me." Because the "something" is so amorphous and undefinable at the moment, it's easier to focus on career.

If a woman is unable to organize her priorities and make a decision she can feel comfortable with, now is the time to look deeper.

4

Feeling "Normal":
Unexamined Assumptions

$\mathcal{M}$ost of us, as women, grow up feeling that we'll inevitably have children someday. For years, we are comfortable with "not yet"; we expect that when we finally have everything in place, motherhood will follow automatically. So it is not surprising that the woman who has reached a point where she is supposed to say "yes," but finds she is not so sure, can feel as if there is something wrong with her. She believes she *should* want to be a mother.

In working with women who are conflicted about motherhood, I have learned that this feeling of "I should" is the major stumbling block to reaching an understanding of the self. It is very frightening to think that there's something wrong or abnormal in your feelings about anything—especially something so intricately woven with our sense of ourselves as women. Isn't motherhood what being a woman is all about?

A woman who is afraid of her negative feelings about motherhood cannot explore them or look at what, in her experience, can make sense of her ambivalence. And since, as I believe, the process of deeply exploring the self in all its complexity *is* the rite of passage that leads to a woman's mature self-definition, I believe all women—the conflicted woman in particular—must explore the unexamined assumptions about women and motherhood that contribute to her sense of "I should want to have a baby."

Primary among these assumptions are that:

- Motherhood is in woman's nature; it is instinctive.
- Motherhood is required to make us feel whole, complete, and fulfilled.

We assume that any normal woman is born with a "maternal instinct" ready to pop up when the time is right and with a built-in guarantee that she will love her baby the minute she lay eyes on it. And we assume that having a baby and caring for it will make us feel like a "normal woman."

Only by pausing to consider these assumptions about "normal" womanhood—where they come from, whose truths they are, and the extent to which they are consonant with her experiences—can a woman reach a point where she is able to define what will feel "normal" *for her.*

What follows is designed to help women take that pause, examine the assumptions that make even the idea of being conflicted about motherhood so fraught with shame, and move beyond a culturally based sense of "normal" to a place where they can freely consider the option of saying "yes" *or* "no," despite the fact that they are now expected to say "yes."

THE CONSTRUCTION OF "NORMAL"

From the time we establish a gendered identity, our understanding of what a "normal" woman naturally is and wants has an enormous influence on the way we approach the choices in our lives and how comfortable we feel with our decisions: this is true of the 4-year-old who wants to wear frilly dresses only; it is true of the 12-year-old who, apprehensive though she may be, impatiently awaits her first menstrual period; it is true of the teenager who yearns to have her first steady boyfriend.

Although the understanding of what a woman is might vary through the life cycle and across cultures, its influence on us does not. As Elisabeth Badinter (1989a) shows in her study of the disastrous effects of wet-nursing among middle-class eighteenth-century French women, in a culture in which a woman's role is defined strictly in relationship to her husband rather than to her baby, it may even be considered normal for a woman to yield up her baby to a nurse for several years with little guarantee that she will see her child again.

From our vantage point, the notion of any woman being so repelled by the sagging breasts and restricted social and sexual life an infant brings is horrifying. That is because we have our own notions of true womanhood. In our society, notions of "the whole woman" and the concept of maternal "instinct," more than any other culturally determined concepts, are at the core of how we feel about ourselves and our bodies—particularly when it comes to motherhood. They are integral parts of every woman's coherent sense of herself by gender—as integral as our knowledge, during girlhood, that sooner or later we will grow breasts, get our periods, fall in love. And as always, there is a standard against which we measure ourselves and against which we are measured: the statistical standard set by "normal" girls and "normal" women.

These standards of normal womanhood become internalized as part of our psychological makeup. Only when we analyze what we have accepted as normalcy can we begin to question its truth. For example, normal women are supposed to experience an urge to mother. But what exactly is this seemingly universal maternal urge? Is it the urge to conceive? The urge to be pregnant? The urge to be a parent?

I always knew I wanted to be a mother. I now know that the urge did not spring out of my genes. It came from my identification with my own mother and with women—that's what women did. When I grew up, I wanted to be like them, and they wanted me to be like them. After all, hadn't my mother given me a Magic Skin doll and a snazzy carriage for her?

I remember being about 4 years old, walking in the park with my friend Emily, both of us wheeling our doll carriages. I remember feeling very grown up, like my mother, saying to my friend Emily as we walked, ". . . and I've been working my fingers down to the bone!" The feeling that I got from saying these totally grown-up, woman words (in exactly my mother's tone) was no less imitative than my desire to have a baby and wheel it in a carriage around the park.

For a long time the most compelling idea for me was to conceive, because that would mean that my body was normal and all my functions were in good working order. My body was something that concerned me. Wanting to conceive wasn't even connected with a desire to be pregnant or to be a mother; I envied my friends who conceived (even those who had abortions). They all had proof that their bodies were normal. They were "normal" women.

Later on, when I yearned for the role of mother, conception itself was less important; what I wanted was a conventional family. If I couldn't grow a baby in my body, I'd adopt. So while the desire for conception *was* purely to do with my body, not with mothering, the urge to parent was not something that had to be expressed by my body. It was a role I wanted, not a universal biological imperative. I knew that even if I could not bear my own child, I would certainly become a mother in whatever way possible.

To me, *grown-up* meant being like my mother—like most women—and becoming a mother one way or another. And because mothering a child was something I desired, something for which I was primed by my experience with cousins, nephews and nieces, and the babies of friends, I knew I would feel comfortable in that role. I cannot say that, had I given birth when I was 20, at a time when I yearned to conceive but was not ready to parent, I would have felt comfortable or intuitive taking care of my infant daughter. But I am certain that I would have felt I belonged to the society of normal, grown-up women.

All our fantasies are influenced by our notions of what is natural for women and what a woman's life is all about. The question is, how valid are these notions for any particular woman? And what of the woman whose fantasies of idyllic motherhood are at odds with the way she actually feels around children, or with the kind of life she feels comfortable leading? As Simone de Beauvoir (1953) articulated, if woman-as-mother is a cultural construction, then—as long as we are aware of the voices influencing our thinking—we can each reconstruct it to make meaningful choices for our own particular lives.

Listening to Cultural Voices

NOTE: A man who has never been a father is not considered less of a man. But a woman who has not mothered is considered less than a whole woman.

Why?

In my practice I often find that making this observation can help a patient embark on an exploration about what it means to be a "real" woman. It is a way of beginning to challenge the shame so many women experience around their ambivalence, a shame that reveals itself in such hesitant comments as, "Maybe I don't really have a good excuse for not having a baby." It is a way of triggering an analysis of cultural precepts that some women can scarcely believe they adhere to (but most women do).

A woman who considers herself truly "liberated" tends to find it hard to admit to herself that deep down inside she still clings to such stereotypical images of what a woman is and wants, or what a woman should be and should want. She needs to understand that these notions are deeply embedded in the very fabric of our culture, shaping the representations of womanhood to which we are all exposed in every area of our lives and throughout our lives. As we internalize them, they become unconscious parts of our thinking. However much we may be conscious of the ways in which society has structured women's experiences in the past, the history of those experiences—the fact that women have for so long found no route to total fulfillment without motherhood—can make it hard for us to extricate ourselves from the spell of "whole" or "natural" womanhood.

THE WHOLE-WOMAN SYNDROME

I believe there is a fallacy in our culture central to many women's conflicts around motherhood, the fallacy that a woman without a child can be defined only by absence. Even the word *childless* conveys a lack. (Increasingly, women who have chosen not to have children and who experience no lack are calling themselves *childfree*.)

Look at the way popular medical and psychiatric literature has characterized women in relation to motherhood. When the youngest child leaves home, the mother must inevitably suffer the "empty nest syndrome." With no children left to mother, what meaning does her life have? When children leave, of course, the separation, psychological and physical, has to be managed. But the empty nest is not the problem—the separation is. This is a rite of passage that both parents and children must go through in order to define themselves anew.

At menopause, when a woman loses the capacity to produce children, she is expected to develop "menopausal depression." Helen Deutsch (1945), an influential disciple of Freud, referred to menopause as woman's "partial death" (p. 459). In fact, the myth of menopausal depression has been debunked by studies showing an inverse correlation between menopause and depressed states of mind, whether or not a woman has a profession (Bernstein and Lenhart 1993). Again, this is a time when many women discover a new sense of freedom in their lives.

Nevertheless, the myths endure, and there's more. . . .

Just as our culture tells us that there is no higher calling, no other raison d'être for a woman than motherhood, it also tells us that mothering is what makes us lesser beings. This double message contributes to the conflict so many women experience and leads to the conclusion that motherhood alone is necessary but not sufficient; you have to have it all.

Woman occupies a paradoxical position in the story of civilization. For as far back as we can see, her capacity to bear and nurture children has been revered, and the idea of woman as mother has been glorified. Yet because of this capacity, woman herself, as the one who mothers, has been relegated to a lowly status. The activities in which motherhood involves her—the messy labor of childbirth and nurturance, the attendance to children—are considered nowhere near as meaningful as man's work out in the world. A woman who has chosen to stay home with her children does not have "whole-person" value.

Options other than motherhood, or as well as motherhood, have been increasingly open to us in the past fifty years. This is due in part to the feminist thinkers of the past half century. Simone de Beauvoir (1953) helped us look more objectively at what it means to be a woman, and especially at the extent to which our feelings about what it means have been shaped by our culture. In the '60s, Betty Friedan (1963) exploded the myth of the "feminine mystique"—that women are, by nature, fulfilled by motherhood. She pointed to the silent problem of her times, finally bringing into the open the fact that the woman who stays home day after day baking cookies with her children and waxing the kitchen floor to an enviable shine might be depressed out of her mind. Her book challenged women to look for new definitions for themselves in the world of work.

In the '70s, Adrienne Rich (1976) questioned the myth of "mother love"—that women automatically love their children, and that the child's best interests are the mother's too. Her book made it easier for women to admit their ambivalence about staying home to raise their kids.

At the same time many women, alienated by what they considered to be '70s feminism's rejection of domesticity, began to sing the virtues of wifedom and motherhood as "caring labor"—surely a more worthwhile endeavor, they proclaimed, than running the rat race.

This message has become a central theme of a popular strain in feminist thought today, which celebrates a unique "woman's sensibility," a "different voice" that rings with the harmony of quintessentially feminine virtues. Women, these theorists suggest, are different from and superior to men because they are selfless, empathic, responsive to the needs of others above their own (Gilligan 1992, Miller 1976).

Certainly woman's biology—her potential for pregnancy and lactation—and her history as childbearer and mother lead her to the idea that she should give of herself. In becoming a parent you must to some degree yield to the needs of a child. Moreover, many women have been brought up to value selflessness to the point that they can feel quite guilty about putting their own interests before or even on a par with another's.

Whether these "feminine" qualities are defined as innate or learned obscures the main issue: to believe that selflessness is a virtue unique to women is to believe that, as a female, you define yourself as a good person through your selflessness. Should you choose not to have children because you cherish your independence, you are selfish and a traitor to the goodness of womanhood; if you decide to be a mother, of course you will want to do everything for your child, no matter how much of yourself you have to sacrifice.

So to be whole you have to have it all: a career to establish your full personhood *and* a child to nurture—and ideally a life partner too. We're increasingly willing to see a woman with a high-powered job but no children as a successful person. But it's not enough to be a person. And if womanliness ultimately means an idealized, selfless motherliness, then the woman who is ambivalent about becoming a mother, or about her role as the mother that she is, is likely to feel less than womanly.

Of course there is still a cultural bias. There is always some bias. If you are not going to have it all, then motherhood is what you should have. Even today, the woman who has a baby but no job is considered more whole than the one who has a job and no baby, because the woman who chooses the baby is considered closer to her nature than the woman who chooses the job. As Deborah Tannen (1992) describes the "Motherhood Bind": "If you're not a Mother, you're a Failed Woman. If you are a Mother, you can't have enough attention to pay to serious work. If you are paying attention to serious work, you must be a Bad Mother" (p. A-19).

Deconstructing "Whole"

"I feel so normal!" a patient of mine exclaimed as she flung herself down on my couch, having just received the test results telling her she was pregnant. She was elated. All her fears about her reproductive functions were quelled. She had conceived, she was fertile, and this made her feel, finally, like a real woman.

"I felt more feminine," another woman told me, describing how she experienced her first pregnancy. There was something about her changing form, her maternal belly, that in her own sense of herself completed her identity as a woman.

"I hated being pregnant," a friend of mine who suffered from interminable morning sickness told me. "But I never felt more alive, more of a woman, than when I was lying in my hospital bed nursing my newborn."

"When I started taking my baby out into the world I felt, for the first time I could remember, completely at peace. It was as if I had joined the sisterhood of women." For this mother of an adopted infant, being a whole woman meant leading a conventional life: pushing her baby in a stroller, sitting on a park bench, and watching her child play. That was what she had grown up believing a woman does, and one adopted child provided her with the fulfillment of that dream.

On the other hand, an orthodox Jewish woman I knew who already had eight children told me she felt inadequate as a woman, because according to the conventions of her particular subculture women are supposed to bear and raise at least twelve—certainly more than ten!

Each of these women identified "womanliness" with some facet of the representation of motherhood as it has been handed down through the generations. Yet, for every one of them, being "whole" meant something slightly different—fertility, maternity, nurturance, conventionality—because within the parameters set by the culture, being "whole" is a purely subjective experience. For some women it means having the biological capacity; adopting a child does not produce a feeling of completion. For others it means having a child to care for, but not necessarily the capacity to bear one. Some women feel at their most womanly during childbirth, but are unhappy with the physical demands of child care and go on to neglect their children. Although pregnancy might feel very satisfying to one mother-to-be, for the woman who regrets her pregnancy, who does not want the child she is carrying, the experience is fraught with shame—not with good feelings about being a true woman.

So what is this motherliness that womanhood apparently depends on? What makes a woman whole?

Redefining "Whole"

Feeling whole is a matter of how you experience yourself and your body. Since it's such a subjective experience, it is variable and open to modification. We can challenge ourselves to rethink our notions of who we are, who we want to be. It is not an absurd notion that we should be acculturated to define ourselves through motherhood. But there are some women who, for any number of reasons, will not be mothers, even to the children they have borne. And not mothering must feel as wholesome for some, *given who they are*, as thoughtfully becoming mothers does for most.

The problem is that when you challenge the motherhood element of woman's traditional self-definition, you throw the rest into a state of upheaval. What *does* make me a woman if I work in a man's world, never use my reproductive capacity, and forgo the womanly route of nurturing a child? How can I feel feminine?

We tend to think of the womanliness-motherliness equation as a universal one, existing not only through history, but also before history and across cultures. It is true that in all societies, across time and across cultures, a person's individual identity is a gendered identity. From a young age you know what being masculine or feminine means in your particular society. It is also true that women everywhere, and across time, have been mothers. But again, by looking at a variety of cultures we can see that the equation of "womanliness" and "motherliness" is not universal; a woman's gendered identity, given different cultural messages, does not inevitably revolve around the experience of motherhood. Even in our own postfeminist culture, women are learning that we can define ourselves as feminine through our gratifying, inti-

mate relationships with others, in the variety of ways we can ne-
gotiate a career, and through the expressions of our sexuality.

As I said before, feeling whole is a subjective experience, and
our subjective experiences of ourselves are modifiable. You could
feel whole as a lover, you could feel whole as a mother. The goal
is really to experience the possibility of choice and the possibility
of change.

THE MYTH OF MATERNAL INSTINCT

Maybe we think of motherhood as natural or "instinctive" for
women because so many women have felt, and do feel, that nurturing babies is fundamental to their fulfillment. For many women
it is. For the woman who feels comfortable with her identification with her mother or a maternal figure in her life, the desire to
have and hold her baby can feel so powerful and "instinctive" that
it has the feel of something inborn. But to suggest that *because*
women have always mothered women are born to mother makes
no sense.

I do not think it is helpful for any woman, in considering motherhood for herself, to think in terms of "instinct" or what's "natural." First, it acts as a bludgeon: for the individual who feels no pull
toward motherhood, what does it mean to say that the desire to
mother is preprogrammed at conception to pop up just at the right
time? It suggests that she, the woman with no yearning to mother,
is unnatural. The implications are that something is wrong with her.

As someone who does not feel driven to nurture a child, a woman
might even tell herself secretly that she is the antithesis of everything "mother" stands for, qualities we have learned to think of as
uniquely feminine, such as selflessness, nurturance, altruism.

Because of the reality of the biological clock, the idea of woman's
"natural" desire to mother can also create considerable anxiety in

a woman who is tending toward choosing a life without children: "What if I wake up when I'm 50 and suddenly feel this drive to have a baby?" is how one of my patients put it.

Most important of all, explaining the urge to mother as "instinctive" blocks all exploration. When we think in terms of instinct we *think* we understand something, and so we look no further. It's genetically programmed; it is inevitable; it's the way it is and has to be; we've evolved this way in the interests of survival. Women naturally want to be mothers, and they're naturally good at it—or should be.

It is not so neat, even in lower animals who do not have the intellectual power to choose.

Take nesting "instinct," for example. All female rats build nests during gestation. That's what female rats do. Why bother to ask why? It fulfills the requirements of "instinct." It is adaptive in the evolutionary sense.

But if you wanted to find out how a rat's life experiences facilitate this nest building—if you were to observe rats in their natural habitat and try to figure out what in their growing up facilitates their nest building—you would see that it does not just happen; it doesn't come "naturally." It is not genetically preprogrammed behavior. Rats must have played with mud, twigs, and leaves before puberty in order for them to make adequate nests for their pups. Of course, these materials are normally found in the early environments of rats, but without such early, playful exposure, pregnant rats will not build nests at the right time (Rosenblatt 1970). This maternal behavior is thus more complicated than any notion of instinct suggests. And if it is this complicated for a rat, how much more so must it be for a human? More than any other animal, our experiences from day one have a massive influence not only on our psychological makeup, but on the very chemistry of our brains.

There are plenty of examples in American ethology (the study of how animals behave in their natural habitats) to show that behaviors we assume are instinctive—such as those associated with mothering—are, in fact, significantly influenced by experience. Ethologists do not, when exploring a behavior exhibited by most members of a species, presume a solely genetic determination; rather, they presume that, given certain reasonably expected environments, "species-typical" behavior emerges.

Applying the term *species typical* to human behavior, we can ask ourselves what, in a particular woman's growing up, sways her toward a life with children or without? Psychologist Nancy Chodorow's (1978) theory on the "reproduction of mothering" from one generation to the next provides a clue: it describes the process whereby a girl's close identification with her mother instills in her psyche the desire to mother. Chodorow, like the ethologists, is talking about a *typical* pattern of individual development.

Defining the desire to mother as species typical encourages us to wonder: To what extent was the environment in which today's woman developed different from those of previous generations? It forces women to explore their conflicts around motherhood as a product, in part, of the gulf between the messages about womanhood they have received from those previous generations and the reality of girls' and women's experiences in the contemporary world. Of course, our grandmothers and their grandmothers accepted that they would inevitably become mothers, and did: getting pregnant *was* a natural fact of their lives. But given a birth-control technology that allows us to efficiently separate sexuality from maternity, today's woman cannot really experience the idea of maternity as a natural part of her life.

Seeing the desire to mother as experientially shaped also throws light on the fact that any number of atypical childhood experiences can (but do not necessarily) interrupt the seamless repetition of mothering from one generation to the next. In my practice I have worked with women who, as children, were entrusted with the care of parents or siblings, women who experienced their own mothers as abusive or neglectful, women whose mothers were severely depressed or who felt terribly ambivalent about their roles as mothers.

By identifying the experiences that led them to question whether they wanted to be mothers themselves, these patients were better able to understand and accept their conflicts and to accept that their mixed feelings about motherhood did not make them any less natural or any less womanly than the woman who cannot wait to care for children of her own.

The word *instinct* will never help us to understand how rich and complex are the experiences that go into the making of maternal desire or behavior, or how variable those desires and behaviors can be. The maternal urge that some women experience— that I experienced—is not in the genes. Mothering behavior is not in the genes. Girls are not born with the urge to mother inside them, ready to appear at the "right" time. What we are born with, if all develops normally, is the *capacity* to reproduce. Only the capacity is a biological given, and clearly that capacity is not essential for a woman to either want to or be able to mother.

We all have to come to terms with what our bodies can and cannot do. We all have to make choices about whether or not to use our inborn capacities. You could have been born with the mental capacity that would allow you to develop a new technology. But will you? It all depends on who you are, who your parents are to you, where you live, what's expected of you or not expected of you, what you're allowed to do, forbidden to do. The capacity is biological, but choice is not, except insofar as our choices are governed by accidents of birth—being born female to a certain family, in a certain culture, at a certain time.

REDEFINING NORMAL:
FEELING COMFORTABLE IN YOUR OWN SKIN

What does normal really mean?

Any definition of "normal" womanhood that relies on being a mother is misleading. "Normal" does not have to reflect a statistical norm. You can be in the minority and nevertheless feel normal, that is to say, feel good about yourself, good enough as a woman, whole. "Normal" is not necessarily "conventional." Being married with two kids is conventional, but trying to conform to that norm will not necessarily make you feel normal—if, for instance, you suffer from severe anxiety or depression because of it.

The novelist Marguerite Duras (1990) spoke once about the place where she lived. It was a seaside town where the normal thing to do was to go to the beach during the day. Most people went.

Duras hated sunbathing. But she wanted to do what everyone else was doing; she wanted to feel normal. So she tried going to the beach in the evening just as everyone else was coming back. "[I]t didn't work. I very much regret having been like that—obeying the rules but never getting any satisfaction out of it" (p. 4). What she *was* good at, she realized, was gazing at the sea. That's what made her feel at one with herself.

What I mean by "normal" is feeling comfortable in your own skin.

You can choose motherhood within a lesbian relationship and feel perfectly normal if you have learned to measure normality by your own inner sense of relative contentment. You can be a single parent and feel more normal than you would living with the wrong partner. You can be a woman without children and feel more at one with yourself than the mother who feels trapped in a role she never really chose.

One woman's "normal" might mean being a professional woman, having a relationship that is an equal partnership, and having a family life. But "family" does not have to mean having your own child.

We can understand what is normal for ourselves by asking: What will allow me to feel most centered and whole with regard to who I am?

Is it having the whole package, a husband and family?

Could I feel normal as a mother whose partner does the nurturing? Might that feel more in keeping with who I am than staying home and minding the baby?

Is it simply having a baby, but not necessarily the man? Could I feel normal as a single mother?

Do I need my own, biological child—the experience of pregnancy and childbirth, and the physical replication of myself? Or do I just need a child to love and raise?

Or can I live the good life childfree?

If I feel I need some contact with children, would I find it enough to be an aunt or a godmother?

It is a matter of the individual woman asking herself certain questions about what "normal" means to her. And because our sense of normal womanhood is mediated primarily through our experiences of our mothers, a woman who is exploring motherhood for herself has to listen to her mother's voice and clarify for herself whether the song it sang was truthful, and whether it rings true for her.

5

Mother's Voices

"Would you want to be a mother like your mother was?"

This is one of the first explorations I make with women who are trying to figure out why they feel ambivalent about motherhood. It is a way of calling up the voice of the person who played the biggest part in defining *mother* for each of us, of making audible the lyrics that play in the most buried parts of ourselves.

To the extent that we identify with our mothers, their voices shape an important part of what being a woman means to us. Inevitably, in communicating what *woman* means, our mothers' voices tell us about the maternal role, both as an ideal and as they in particular have experienced it.

I want to talk about each woman's unique experience of her particular mother *as a mother*—both the person we know as adults and especially the one we remember from our childhoods. I believe that for each of us some part of our image of mother and of ourselves as women with or without children is inextricably bound up with the nature of this experience.

Here we'll look at the difficult, sometimes painful task of exploring that experience by making audible your mother's voice from your early childhood. The purpose of this endeavor is to move toward an objective understanding of her as a woman. Making her voice audible is often a very difficult task for several reasons. Primary among them is the fact that a woman's feelings about how she was mothered and about the woman who mothered her are embedded in her psychic structure at an early age. Being internalized, our mother's voice can feel like our own. It is deeply buried, so much a part of us it can be very hard to reveal.

Listening to our mother's voice becomes even harder when the lyrics we remember hearing were inconsistent or untrue, or were not lyrics she really spoke or even lyrics she would have wanted to write. Mothers have complex roles that, as women in their world, they approach with all of their own personal complexity. Children, who are not yet ready to understand such complexity, tend to simplify. These simplifications are distortions of what was real. The first task of the conflicted woman, then, is to examine who her mother really was, and to try to reconstruct a reasonable truth from the tangle of maternal and childish distortions.

Only by being more objective, by being as realistic about her mother as possible, can a woman begin to distinguish for herself the ways in which she is the same as, as well as different from, her. And only then can she measure her mother's voice against her current sense of herself and ask herself, "Do I want to be a different kind of mother? Do I need to be? Can I be different enough to be my own kind of mother—or not be a mother at all?"

DO I WANT TO BE A MOTHER?

I have noticed that, when getting acquainted, people usually ask, "Do you have children?" not, "Are you a mother?" Because this is the way we tend to phrase the question, women, in their conflicts around motherhood, usually ask themselves, "Do I want to have a baby? Is there room for a child in my life?" and, "What will it mean if I never have a child?"

Calling Up Mother's Voices

Although these questions are useful ones, I have found in my work that the most meaningful question, the one that produces the most productive responses, is: "Do I want to be a mother?" This is the question that can help a woman call up that early voice and make the link between what she hears and how she feels at this moment in her life about assuming the role of the woman who mothered her and who created her primary image of motherhood.

Sandy's Story

The story of a woman named Sandy illustrates my point. When Sandy came to see me, her analyst of many years had just died, and she wanted me to help her bring her treatment to a close or refer her to a new therapist.

Sandy, a very smart, forthright lawyer, was 40 when we met. After a few months, our work of coping with her analyst's death ended. She left with the understanding that I would continue to be a resource for her. She reappeared five years later. She had finally settled down and married. Mindful of her biological clock, she and her husband had decided it was time to start a family. Shortly thereafter, her husband had discovered that he was infertile. They toyed briefly with the idea of trying artificial insemination with a chosen friend's semen, but decided, without much ado, "Why bother?" They were so focused on whether or not to "have a baby" that the question of adoption never even came up.

When Sandy came in this time, she was terribly confused by the fact that she had been finding herself, in her late forties, following baby carriages. What was going on? She had a good marriage, was happy in her job; her life was fine and she certainly thought she had made peace with the idea of not having a child. Or had she?

During that first catch-up session, I remarked to Sandy that, although she had answered the question, "Do I want to have a baby?" she had never asked herself, "Do I want to be a mother?"

At which Sandy promptly burst out crying.

"This must be important," she said through her tears. "You must have touched something really important."

And so began Sandy's journey of exploration.

Realizing that she had never dealt with her conflicts around the maternal role, Sandy immediately began talking about her mother who, she said, had not really enjoyed mothering. Her father, a lawyer like Sandy, was the one who would get down on the floor and play with the children, the one who could be cuddly and wacky. Her mother, whose parents' suffering during the Depression had made them unavailable to her, found it hard to relate to the fun part of parenting, only to the daily grind.

As she talked, Sandy began to see that, though she loved her mother, she did not want to identify with her mother's role. How could she? The way she saw it, it was nothing but drudgery. No wonder she had so easily put aside the idea of having a baby. Had she at that time asked herself whether she wanted to be a mother, she would at least have had to deal with the conflicts that the evocation of "mother" brought to light. Who knows what she would have decided, but she would have been resolved earlier.

To Sandy's question, "Why now?" there were no good, quick answers. Clearly, something in her psyche had shifted. The desire for a biological child had receded; the desire to assume the role of mother—which she had never examined before—had taken over. She left my office pondering the motherhood question in a new way.

A couple of months later Sandy called me to say that she and her husband were adopting twins.

Sandy was a seasoned, self-aware patient with an understanding of therapy as a process and a sharp, analytical mind. It is not usually so easy to isolate your mother's voice and recognize the ways in which it underlies your puzzling conflicts. In most cases, calling up that voice takes a thorough exploration of your experiences as a child of the woman who mothered you, and of your mother as a woman who had her own life separate from yours, both inside and outside the home—the woman who was married to your father, who worked or did not work, who had her own friends, and, of course, who had her own mother.

Certain questions can help women embark on this process of exploration:

Do I want to be like my mother? As a whole person? As a woman? As a wife? As a mother?
Would she expect me to? Would she approve of me if I did?
Do I feel I *ought* to be like her?
Did she like being a mother?

When I think, "This is how I ought to be" as a person, woman, wife, mother, how much of that "ought" is my mother's voice speaking in me?

When I imagine what it feels like to be a mother, how much of my imagining is based on my mother's experience as I perceived it?

The point is, our "oughts" about motherhood tend to reflect what, deep down, we believe our mothers were, what they wanted for themselves, and what they wanted us to be and do. And our fantasies about ourselves as mothers—good or bad, happy or frustrated—are created around our perceptions of how our mothers felt in their roles. The maternal lyrics we hear, and therefore the way we imagine ourselves as mothers or cannot imagine it, are a product of who our mothers were to us, or who we felt they wished they could be, or what they wanted for us.

WHEN MOTHER'S VOICE IS MUDDLED

Our mothers are our first role models, our first world. As infants we believe we *are* our mothers; growing into girls, we tend to continue to see ourselves as the same as they are. As beings of the same gender, they tell us what a woman's life is about, both in the way they live their lives and in what they communicate to us verbally and nonverbally as they nurture us. Their experiences, as we perceive them, inform our earliest expectations of ourselves. Their voices tell us, "Be like me."

What happens when what we hear is muddled? Different from what we're seeing? False?

What if the voices we hear now were created by the child who interpreted her mother's behavior, her passing frowns and smiles and casual comments, and put it all together in a certain way?

What if we misinterpreted? For example, I have had in my practice patients whose fathers died when they were very young, and who had to deal with mothers who were preoccupied and often depressed. In the children's minds, they were mothers who simply did not love them—and to the children, this meant that they themselves were unlovable.

What happens when what we hear is inconsistent? When our mother's experiences seem to shift from positive to negative and back? When their roles and experiences change dramatically in the course of our growing up? When they want something different from what they have? When they want for their daughters something other than what they themselves have?

Instead of a single, clear, maternal voice, we end up with a cacophony of voices emanating from one powerful source and dispensing mixed messages about motherhood. I would say that these mixed maternal messages—many of which arise from maternal ambivalence around and idealization of the mothering role—are one of the main causes of conflict in women who are considering motherhood today.

Daughters of Ambivalent Mothers

Many mothers of the '60s and '70s were highly ambivalent about their roles. Child-care literature of the time stressed the importance of full-time maternal care; feminist literature was encouraging women to be more than "just mothers"; the voices of tradition told mothers they should feel contented with their picture-perfect domestic lives. Unable to acknowledge or understand their conflicts because "good mothers" were not supposed to be conflicted, their negative and therefore guilty feelings expressed themselves in all kinds of ways ranging from anger to denial to detachment, often including a resentful self-sacrifice whose subtext is a sense of feeling deprived: "Where's my life?"

One woman told me: "My mother baked cookies with us and did all the things a mother was supposed to do. On the one hand she was very happy—having children was definitely something she wanted to do. But on the other hand she let us know how much she was sacrificing in order to give us that. I got a sense from her of what a rotten job mothering could be—that you never get back what you put in. The way I saw it, though she loved us she didn't really feel good in the role of nurturer; it just wasn't her thing, and it stopped her doing the things she would have liked to do, things for herself. So I worry I'll feel that way too."

It can be terribly confusing for the contemporary woman, whose contemporary voices—including, quite possibly, the real mother of her grown-up life—tell her, "You can have it all," and yet whose image of motherhood is of a life consumed by diapers and floor wax.

Mothers can lie.

Because of the messages our mothers received about motherhood being every woman's true destiny, they may have told both their children and themselves one thing—"It's the most wonderful experience in the world"—while communicating nonverbally a far less wonderful sense of frustration, wistfulness for opportunities lost, even bitterness or at least regret. The greater the mother's lie, the more difficulty her daughter is likely to experience in clarifying her conflicts around motherhood.

Mothers can forget.

One woman, writing in a literary magazine, remembers from her early childhood her mother's screaming complaints about how she couldn't stand it, how her children had ruined her life. Yet the mother she now speaks with—the mother of her adult life—denies any such feelings. "Of course she denies it: what she did then, she could not control; something buried deep inside her, so deep and so unattended that all it could do was fester, drove her to act this way. Maybe she really doesn't remember. . . . For me, for many years, having a child meant being condemned to live a long, painful lie" (Maloney 1993, p. 20).

Because a mother's voice can change with time, because an ambivalent mother may have sung two different lyrics on a single day, because our mothers may have lied or failed to cover the feelings of which they were ashamed, it is imperative that a woman listen with the utmost care to all of her mother's voices—not only to the idealized lyrics mothers would like their children to remember, but also to those that are most muffled in both the mother's and the daughter's memories.

Hearing Ambivalent Voices

I think it is important for any woman looking at her own mother to see her as a product of her particular familial, social, and historical contexts no less than she, the daughter, is a product of her own context. It is often easier to tease out a mother's various voices, and less painful to accept that our mothers may have been ambivalent, if we can understand that our mothers' choices and compromises were governed by what was possible and what was not possible for them. What were the forces impinging upon her that made her ambivalent? What were the strictures that made it necessary for her to save face by lying or deceiving herself about the conflicting pulls she experienced? What was the ideal of motherhood against which she measured herself, and possibly found herself lacking?

Often our more conscious perceptions of our mothers are based on the relationships we have developed with them during our adult years. Recapturing the voice of our early mother—recalling our childhood experience of her—can make her a real and complicated lady. Women can ask themselves questions like:

Did she enjoy being a mother?
How dependent was she on her role as mother for her sense of
    herself?
How much did the demands of motherhood compromise her
    sense of herself?
What else besides her children was meaningful to her?

Reaching back to your mother's early voice is a matter of examining your memories of the mother of your childhood, in as objective a way as possible, from your current perspective as a mature woman. To be truly objective, it is important to retain a healthy skepticism in the face of your current sentiments about motherhood. It is also important to remember that our mothers may have their own needs to defend the lives they led, or to see us as happy mothers and thereby see themselves as successful ones. Women must be careful to read between the lines of the stories they have created or heard about their early childhoods. We must allow ourselves to see the mother of our past as a complex individual who may have had pulls that conflicted with her desire to mother her children, and who may have felt terribly ashamed of those pulls.

The Idealized Mother versus the Real Mother

It took the poet and feminist Adrienne Rich (1976) fifteen years to find the equanimity to record, in *Of Woman Born*, her experiences as a '50s and early '60s mother—to "dare to return to a ground which seemed to me the most painful, incomprehensible, and ambiguous I had ever traveled, a ground hedged by taboos, mined with false namings" (p. 15).

Rich, who in becoming a mother had simply done what women did, felt devastated by the feelings that her role aroused in her. She wrote in her diary about how her children's voices "fill me with despair at my own failures, despair too at my fate, which is to serve a function for which I was not fitted" (p. 21). That "function," as Rich perceived it then—as it was perceived and represented by the culture-at-large—was to provide unconditional love, to "treasure the invisible thread that binds child to mother," to "yield wholeheartedly to a singular, maternal identity" (p. 21). There was no room in this definition for a woman's desire to be and feel like something other than a mother.

Rich's story shows not only what mothers have been up against in terms of their sense of self, but also how important it is to look carefully at the image of motherhood against which you have been comparing the mother you imagine you might be (or could never be). Is this image realistic? Where does it come from? Is it the same image that might have plagued your mother? The image that made *her* feel ashamed because she was unable to be the selfless, ever-patient, unconditionally loving mother mandated by her culture? The image, nevertheless, she felt compelled to communicate?

Children are willing accomplices in this idealization. Most of us as young children tend to see our mothers as the most beautiful, the best, the most loving. Especially if we remain close to our mothers as adults, the process of gaining a true picture of their struggles, their failings, can be a very difficult one.

FEAR OF BECOMING YOUR MOTHER

Once in a while a patient comes to me who, for reasons she cannot fully understand, is torn between wanting very much to have a child and being terrified of becoming a mother. Her terror might arise from the fact that when she is around children she feels mean, distant, impatient, or anxious. She might be consciously aware that her response to children in some way replicates or reacts against her mother's, or she might be entirely unconscious of it. She might feel perfectly comfortable around children, yet when she imagines herself a mother to her own child she sees herself as her mother and is stopped short. My job is to help such a woman accept that, first, her feelings will ultimately make sense to her, and second, the understanding of *how* they make sense will provide her with the option of having control over how she feels.

Making Sense of Your Feelings

Our lives are not open books. We remember some things, but a great deal is buried. Even if we do remember, we do not necessarily connect our history with who we have become. As long as we are reasonably content, we do not have to look for the unconscious underpinnings of our feelings or behaviors. The woman who wants to be a mother and enjoys children does not have to question why she enjoys them.

But when something we feel or do is conflictual for us, we have to take a deeper look at why, because, whatever the reason, it made sense for us at some point in our lives to feel or behave that way. If we can discover why it made sense in the past, we can free ourselves to ask whether it still does. Making sense of it can be a difficult and extremely painful process, sometimes impossible to work through without professional help—especially if there has been any trauma involved. The important thing to remember is that there are good reasons for the way we feel.

The story of a patient of mine, Delia, sheds some light on how we are able to unbury what we have purposefully buried from our childhood experiences and thereby make sense of a behavior that was once psychologically useful, though it might create conflict in the present. It is the story of a woman who, because she had so idealized her mother, could not fathom why *she* was afraid of becoming a mother in turn. As long as she continued not seeing her mother as a real person she could not hope to understand her fear. It tells of her struggle to understand her fear by listening to her mother's voice, thus discovering the gap between the real and the ideal.

Delia's Story

Delia came into therapy believing that she had been raised by a perfect mother. The two of them had developed a wonderful friendship during her adult life. They were like two peas in a pod. Delia had in many ways designed a life that was a mirror of her mother's—they were even in similar professions: Delia was a physician, her mother was a research scientist in a related health field.

It was very important for Delia to be the kind of woman her mother was. She felt immensely comfortable following in her footsteps when it came to the way she dressed, the profession she chose, the ballets and operas she adored. And yet, when it came to the question of nurturing a small child, those same footsteps stopped abruptly and left her in a state of panic. She felt she wanted children, yet was very afraid that she would be a bad mother. Delia was so afraid that she was paralyzed.

Why was this?

One day I asked Delia, "If you were to be a mother, would you want to be the same kind of mother yours was?"

Her response—an emphatic "No!"—stunned her. Why would she say that? How could she possibly feel this way?

So we talked about Delia's childhood. I had sensed that all had not been so idyllic in her early childhood. There was a fogginess in her recall of those years. The picture was too rosy in places, blank in others. A piece of the story was missing.

And yet how could it be? Her mother, as she experienced her now, was the best in the world!

I told Delia a folktale about a little girl who got lost at the fairground. When she was asked what her mother looked like, she said, "She is the most beautiful mother in the world." Everybody went searching the fairground for the fantastically beautiful mother of this child, to no avail. Finally, an extremely ugly, hunched, and tattered woman came by, frantically searching for her lost child. The little girl spotted her and ran into her arms.

"See!" she cried out, "Didn't I tell you she was the most beautiful mother in the world!"

Delia struggled every step of the way to retain her image of the perfect mother. In helping her become more objective, I encouraged her to recognize that if we love an idealized object, our love does not have the depth that the love for a real person, warts and all, has.

I reminded her of a story she had told me about how her mother had once been so "out to lunch" she forgot Delia's sister in her baby carriage at the supermarket and went home. She had laughed at the story as if it had become a family joke; I pointed out that this story was not really very funny. I suggested that perhaps her mother had been a little distracted.

Delia assured me that her mother had loved her children, and that the moment she had realized her mistake, she had gone rushing back to fetch the baby from the supermarket.

I told Delia: "I'm sure she loved her children. But how would you feel if you were a mother who was so distracted she forgot her baby in a supermarket?" After all, I reminded her, although everything worked out okay, her mother had lost track of her child. It had to have some relevance to Delia's feelings about being a mother.

"You really think so? My mother was really a very good mother," Delia insisted.

As Delia started to become more thoughtful about her childhood over time, she began to recall some wretched moments. In fact, her childhood had often been an unhappy one. But she attributed this to the caregiving provided by her paternal grandmother while her mother was busy with her work. Delia described her grandmother as very harsh, a woman who would literally wash out the children's mouths with soap and water. Delia had been afraid of her.

I asked Delia if her mother had been aware of any of this.

"Of course not," she answered. "I never told her. It would have made her angry and upset. How was she to know what went on?"

I asked Delia if she would want to be the kind of mother who doesn't know what is going on with her children day to day.

Delia continued to insist that her mother was a very good mother to her and her sister.

I suggested to Delia that those quite possibly isolated incidents when her mother had been "out to lunch" could have figured very powerfully in her experience as a daughter.

I wanted Delia to understand that all through her life she had sheltered herself, and her mother too, from the knowledge of how scarring those early years had been. Anything else would have forced them both to face the fact of the mother's detachment and distractibility. Somehow Delia had always known that her mother needed to be reassured that she was a good parent. She felt that it was her job to calm her mother's anxiety about mothering. Her sister was the troublemaker; she was the well-oiled wheel. By not making her mother anxious, by not revealing how unhappy she was with the grandmother, she could please her. So her idealization had served her well—until now.

I told Delia: "Though your mother was clearly loving and is a wonderful woman in many ways, there must have been something in her mothering that left a frightening imprint, because the notion of being exactly like her horrifies you." I explained to her that though her mother was not a bad mother, she wasn't perfect. No mother is perfect. In Delia's mind as a child, given her particular sensitivities at that time and the normal vulnerability experienced by young children, the fact that her mother could sometimes be "out to lunch" made her feel terribly unprotected and terribly frightened. As I told Delia, in her mind as a child, that translated as "sometimes my mother is a bad mother."

Gradually Delia was able to fill in a realistic portrait of her mother, a mother who had been at times so absorbed in her work that she could give only half her attention to her children. When her mother was "there," she was very there, but when she was not. . . . Even now, Delia often had the sense when talking with her mother on the phone that at times she was listening, but not hearing. Her mind was somewhere else. But when Delia would ask her if she'd heard, she would say, "Of course! I heard every word."

SEEING YOURSELF AS YOUR OWN WOMAN

In struggling toward an honest appraisal of her feelings about motherhood and an objective sense of who her mother really was, and is, a woman enters the process of becoming her own person.

The process begins with an evaluation of how the mother's moment in history, her circumstances and who she is contributed to her issues as a parent. You can determine the ways in which your historical moment and circumstances are different from hers. And you can look at those parts of yourself that remind you of her.

By uncovering Delia's deeply buried perception of her early mothering as occasionally "bad," or at least neglectful, we found the key to her fear that she might not be a good mother should she choose to have a child. And when she was finally able to say, "My mother could be distracted. My mother could be negligent. She should have known what was going on," Delia could ask, "Will I have to be that kind of mother, or can I be different?" To the extent that her mother's distractibility signified to her that this was a woman who had not really loved being a mother to very young children, she also had to ask herself, "Will I feel more comfortable than she did caring for a child? What was there in her history, and in who she was that made mothering difficult for her, that does not hold true for me?"

It was a turning point for Delia. We talked about the ways in which she was different from her mother and the ways in which she was the same. Delia had felt compelled to be like her mother as a way of gaining her approval in competition with her siblings. And indeed, like her mother, Delia wanted to do what was conventional within her particular world. She had been expected and expected herself to get educated, get married, and have a family. Also like her mother, a profession was very important to Delia.

What liberated her to imagine having a child was her understanding of why she needed to be the same and how she could in fact be different. She did not have to be like her mother in all ways. As I reminded her, being able to identify what she had found so troublesome in her mother's parenting brought her one step closer to avoiding a repetition.

Becoming a Different Kind of Mother

Women whose mothers, rather than becoming preoccupied with the nonmaternal, occupied themselves exclusively with the maternal and ended up resenting the sacrifice they made, can also ask themselves, "How am I different from my mother? How can I be a different kind of mother?"

They can ask themselves:

How can I avoid feeling the way she felt?

Did she make a real choice about becoming a mother or did she "just do it"?

And if I choose motherhood, acknowledging some mixed feelings, will I be able to live with those feelings without becoming resentful?

Can I shape the job to fit my needs, knowing what those needs are? If I know that, like my mother, I'd go crazy staying home with a child twenty-four hours a day, can I be a happier mother than she was by staying in my job full time and hiring a nanny?

Maybe your mother's voice tells you, "There's only one way to be a mother, and that's the way I did it—full time." And yet you do not feel that way. Some women worry that they do not feel nurturant enough to care for a baby, or believe that their commitment to a career is a powerful argument against motherhood. I would argue again that our assumptions about women as nurturers are culturally based. Nurturance is usually associated with women. It's a message that is internalized: "You have to be nurturant to be a good mother, and only you, as the mother, can be the nurturer."

My point is that instead of asking herself, "Can I be a nurturant enough mother?" a woman can ask, "Will my child receive nur-

turant enough parenting? Can my partner/mother/sister/baby-sit-
ter supplement the loving care that I can give comfortably on a
part-time basis?"

Delia knew she would have to find a nurturant caregiver to be
with her child while she worked, and that she would have to know
that things were really okay while she was gone. But she also
needed to know that *she* could be a nurturing figure in her child's
life. Two experiences helped her to see herself as someone who
could be this kind of mother. She liked the way she was with her
friends' children, and, as she watched their parents—her friends—
struggle to become the kinds of mothers and fathers they wanted
to be, she began to believe that she could do at least as well.

Detaching from a Damaging Mother

Many women experience a vague discomfort when they imagine
that, in becoming mothers, they might be or feel like their own
mothers. Women who experienced their mothers as unhappy or
unavailable can be quite fearful about reproducing their roles and
have to work harder at recognizing their separate identities. But
for the woman who grew up with a mother who was abusive,
unloving, or dysfunctional, grappling with the question of whether
to have a child involves much more than seeing herself as a different kind of mother from her own or motherhood as a different
kind of role than the one her mother defined for her. Like Delia,
who could not understand why she was so afraid of becoming a
mother, she might not understand her fear as the fear of reproducing her mother's mothering.

One patient of mine knew only that she was afraid because every
time she found herself around children she became mean. She
thought she was a "bad" person, not fit to be a mother. In therapy
she was able to link her experience of her mother as "hateful" and
her hateful feelings around children, to understand that something

in the repetition of the mother–child relationship as she had experienced it chilled her to the bone. In fact, her avoidance of children had made good sense for much of her life. With this knowledge she could struggle very hard to understand that becoming a mother need not doom her to becoming *her* mother. It is a struggle from which, I believe, all conflicted women can learn something, even if their childhood experiences of "mother" were actually relatively benign.

I remember a story a supervisor of mine told me that has become emblematic in my work with patients. To demonstrate how problematic behaviors were once valuable, he told me the following: a man went into therapy because he had a phobia of going underground. He was unable to use the subway, and needed to do so for his first job out of college. Surface transit, which had served him in the past, would no longer do.

It was only during therapy that this man recalled having been sexually molested in a church basement during his boyhood. His avoidance of underground spaces had initially protected him from having to relive that traumatic experience. At the time, in other words, his never descending into subterranean places made good, adaptive sense for him. But now, as an adult, it only made his life impossible.

How could he get over his fear?

His therapist suggested a mantra that he could use whenever he had to enter the subway:

"A subway is not a church.

"A subway is not a church.

"A subway is not a church."

I believe this is a motto for all of us. It calls upon a new voice that is able to discriminate, through an understanding of one's history, between the needs of a past self and the needs of a present self, and also between the source of the original injury and whatever has become identified with it.

Whatever a woman's automatic response to children or to the very idea of motherhood, there are questions that can be asked. If she came into adulthood hating herself around children, she should not dismiss it as her "craziness" or "badness." She has to respect that at one time it meant emotional survival for her; it was her way of adapting to her childhood world while she evolved as a functioning individual. She would not have learned to dislike children if it had not made some good psychological sense.

Women who are fearful need to tell themselves: "Something about my past makes sense of how I feel. What was it?"

By becoming conscious of what this something was, by realizing, "That's what it's about!" a woman who feels uncomfortable around children or afraid of the idea of herself as a mother can look at her contemporary life and see that her way of feeling, which once made sense, may no longer serve her well. She does not need to be that way any more. Just as the phobic man could tell himself, "A subway is not a church," the woman who is afraid of repeating her mother's experience can tell herself, "I am not my mother," or whatever other appropriate mantra can free her to consider what is right for her now.

I do not want to suggest here that every woman who has rejected or hesitated about motherhood because of something negative in her own childhood experience should examine this so she can become a mother. She might still have good reasons for remaining childless, or she might not want to repeat her mother's journey even though she understands that she could be a much better parent. But whether or not she chooses to try, I believe she should know, within herself, that she does have the option.

Ultimately, we all make a choice to be like our mother as a mother, to be a different kind of mother than our mother was, or to be a different kind of woman—not a mother at all. By going through the process outlined here, a woman enables herself to choose which of these paths is best for the woman she has become in her own right, in her own time.

6

Choosing Again . . . and Again: Infertility

$\mathcal{A}$ woman struggles to make a choice about motherhood. She decides: Yes, she wants to have a baby. But she does not conceive. Once again she is faced with a choice. Where once she asked herself, "Do I want to be a mother?" now she has to ask, "How much do I want it? How hard do I try?"

She can "pick up the gauntlet," feel challenged, and turn her now unequivocal desire for a child into a campaign. If so, she will have to think about how strong for her is the pull of biological as opposed to adoptive motherhood.

Or, having defined herself as a woman who will mother, can she now redefine herself? Can she say, knowing all the routes to motherhood available, that childlessness for her need not be by default—"I could not"—but by conscious choice—"I will not."

Whatever her initial feelings about her infertility, a woman has to explore again her choice for motherhood. She has to look anew at what it means to her to be in control of her body and her life; she has to ask herself, again, what "whole" or "natural" woman means to her. And she has to look at how her definition of *mother* has been shaped by her own mother. I believe it is of the utmost importance that she ask herself these questions again at every juncture of the campaign, after each disappointment, after each failure to conceive or adopt.

Then, once again, the conflicted woman has to balance her fear of regret against the risks involved. But now the stakes are higher. Once, the risk of regretting a "no" seemed to outweigh the risks involved in saying "yes." How does that balance shift when she adds to "yes" the risks and compromises that come with all medical and legal procedures, and of course the significant financial costs of both?

The following pages explore this process. But first of all, they explore the initial sense of loss most women experience when they first discover that what they had always assumed would happen at the right time won't happen. Not every woman experiences this loss the same way. It depends on how you have come to the decision to be a mother and with what fantasy of self-fulfillment.

INFERTILITY AS LOSS: A SPOILED IDENTITY

Infertility comes as a devastating shock to the woman who has chosen motherhood. Whatever her feelings about herself as a potential mother, when she discovers that she is infertile she has to contend with loss. Even if she fully believes she will be able to become a mother somehow, in various ways she is likely to experience some assault on her sense of self.

First, the infertile woman might experience loss with regard to her feeling like a "natural" or "real" woman. One woman told me, "Being fertile means being able to do what a woman is supposed to do. When you find out you aren't for whatever reason, it becomes a mourning process."

Especially if she has postponed motherhood, the woman who discovers that she cannot do what a woman is supposed to do has to deal with a loss of her sense of being in control of her bodily functions. She might feel helpless; her feeling of being in charge of her life might be compromised. Along with this, the woman who has postponed very often experiences a blow to her sense of her own competency as a modern woman for whom everything seemed possible. And she might blame herself for what, in her mind, she has brought upon herself.

If a woman has based her sense of herself around the assumption that she will be a mother someday, the possibility that this may not happen forces her to reconsider herself in all the facets of her current and future life. How these realignments work out depends to a large extent on how central motherhood is to her self-definition.

Fertility and "Real Womanhood"

A woman who discovers that she has problems with her fertility has to acknowledge that motherhood, which was supposed to be a birthright, a natural fact-of-woman, is not going to happen the way it was supposed to—"naturally"—and perhaps not at all.

Why does this feel so devastating?

What does infertility mean for a woman's definition of herself?

Given all the new technological possibilities that exist in assisted reproductive technology, we have to ask ourselves what exactly infertility means. After all, the infertile woman can now consider herself functionally fertile. Even though she may still feel infertile (or at least different from other women who do not have to undergo technological manipulations to bear their own children), she need not be "barren"—or so she is told.

Adria Schwartz (1994), in an essay entitled "Taking the Nature Out of Mother," makes the point that high-tech reproductive technologies have liberated women from the idea of "natural womanhood."

Theoretically at least, these technologies do force us to question not only the meaning of fertility, but also the meaning of womanhood, and of motherhood. Writes Schwartz: "The associative link between women, fertility, and motherhood is being eroded, if not broken, in the laboratory. The traditional shame of barrenness, the inevitable sterility of menopause, the onerous ticking of the biological clock, the very legitimization of womanhood by reproductive function, are all called into question by alternative modes of reproduction" (p. 242).

In fact, given the technology that has been developed, it is hard to say what "fertility" really means. The French feminist philosopher Elisabeth Badinter (1989b) observes that, "When several women participate in the reproductive process, how is it possible to determine which one shall be called 'fertile'? In the case of 'shared motherhood,' is the woman fertile who gives the egg, or is it the one whose womb receives the embryo?" (p. 189). And of course, which woman is the real mother? The one who donates the egg, or the one who carries the embryo and bears the child? As Adria Schwartz (1994) asks in a subheading of her essay, "Will the Real Mother Please Stand Up?" (p. 241).

Certainly the implications of the new reproductive technologies can help us toward new definitions of woman and her fertility—redefinitions that first emerged with the widespread use of contraception. But ironically, though on many levels we are able to separate our sexuality from our capacity to reproduce and our femininity from our reproductive functions, the very existence of this technology and the possibilities it affords us serve to reinforce the traditional association between whole womanhood and woman as biological mother. Seduced by the promise that she can be "fertile," the middle-class woman diagnosed with fertility problems might put off even thinking about adoption—let alone a life without children—until she has exhausted, or is exhausted by, the "high-tech" route, a period that can span several years.

Given all the new choices that present themselves as well as the pressures to pursue a biological route to motherhood, an infertile woman must examine what *woman* and *mother* mean to her more energetically than she might have had to before:

Do I have to feel ashamed of my infertility—if it is my problem and not my husband's?

Do I have to feel barren?

Would I feel comfortable becoming a mother by function only, were I to adopt a child? Or is my will to become a mother connected with the physical experience, the blood tie? Why?

Can I feel that my body is womanly enough on the basis of my sexuality? Or does my association of "motherly" and "womanly" hinge on bodily images of pregnancy, birth, and breast feeding?

Do I imagine that I could bond only with a biological child?

And do I see mother love as inevitable, given a biological child, even though I also know that not all mothers—biological or adoptive—manage to form such bonds.

How do I feel comparing myself to my older sister, who has a sensational child who looks just like her?

How do I feel with regard to my mother? What are her expectations for me? How would she feel about my choices?

Loss of the Whole Body

We started this journey looking at how the idea of choosing "yes" about motherhood is scary because it implies a loss of the control we have come to value. One important aspect of that loss is control over the body. The woman who has decided to have a baby has accepted that loss—at least as a transient condition. Now she comes face to face with it in a new way. Having spent years controlling her fertility, she realizes she has no control. Where once she could assume a level of control because she trusted in the integrity of her body, now that trust is broken.

Although we tend to experience any physical injury as a narcissistic blow, infertility just seems more powerful. In the experience of many infertile women, you become less than you were, less than you are supposed to be, and less than every other normal woman who can become a mother with her own body if and when she wants to. Your woman's body is lacking something essential to it. You are not a "normal" woman. You are not whole. Or so it seems.

A 39-year-old woman told me: "I've been in shock the last couple of months as it's dawned on me that I might not be able to have children. A part of me feels that there's something wrong with my persona, like when you get cancer or you get raped. Something makes you feel so different, so much less than a whole person."

Even the woman who has never experienced her reproductive functions as central to her womanhood can experience a sense of irretrievable loss. "I felt betrayed by my body," another woman said. "It was scary that something wrong went on inside my body that I couldn't feel. And I wondered what else was going on in there that I couldn't feel was wrong."

Not Having It All

More and more in the contemporary world a woman's infertility also implies a loss of the sense she had of herself as a woman for whom everything is possible. In my experience with patients the woman who has postponed childbearing to pursue a career, always expecting that in the end she will "have it all," has a particularly hard time adjusting her definition of herself.

A friend of mine told me: "I always thought I was going to do everything. I was going to build my career, I was going to make a home, and I was going to make a baby. When you discover you're infertile your grandiosity gets shot down. That powerful creature you thought you were—suddenly you're not."

My friend, like so many women of her generation, had always believed that she was truly in control of her life. She was in charge of her own future, and if she worked hard enough at getting what she wanted, she could have it. The woman's movement had made the American dream as available to her as to her brother. But her body had put it beyond her reach.

In our grandmothers' day infertility was a shame and made you less of a woman. You could not "provide" your husband with a child, and there were few other means of expressing oneself as a woman. Today an infertile woman is likely to feel less valued because she is not everything she could be, everything she has learned to feel entitled to be. She can no longer value herself for herself as she could when she imagined her body was whole and the world was hers.

Another friend, Penny, did not discover that she was infertile until, at the age of 37 and newly married, she and her husband started "trying" to have a baby. After a year of not conceiving she underwent a medical workup and discovered that her fallopian tubes were blocked, probably from a silent pelvic inflammatory disease contracted when she was much younger.

"I was in shock," she said. "My husband was in shock." They had married because they both wanted to start a family. Motherhood was something Penny wanted very much, not because her life would be otherwise empty—she felt fulfilled in a loving marriage and in her role as a tenured professor of French literature—but because it would augment the fullness of her life. Penny told me: "The more things worked in the other parts of my life, the more certain I felt that it was possible to have everything."

The Wages of Sin

These feelings of lost identity and lost control may be compounded by guilt. Having waited for "the right time," the postponer finally discovers that her body will not do what she fully expected of it for so long—and what it might already have done once already, before the time was right. It is not uncommon for women who have postponed motherhood, and who had an abortion earlier in life, to see their infertility as "just desserts."

"You think, I had that abortion at 25—I could have had a 15-year-old kid by now," another woman told me. "I don't believe in God, but anyway you start to think, am I being punished somehow?"

Having grown up with one code of female sexual morality and come of age when a more liberated one was blossoming, some women who once saw themselves as progressive and sexually free now look back and wonder if they were really "loose" or "bad girls." And weren't we always told that bad girls would pay in the end? "My mother was right after all."

A woman might blame herself not only for the abortion she had when she was younger, but also for the sex she enjoyed with boyfriends, for having been on the pill or having used an IUD, for the cigarettes she smoked, the drugs she took—in short, for all the things her mother or grandmother would not have approved of.

She might blame herself not only for her sexuality, but also for having been swept up by feminist notions of success and self-development. In fact, all that creativity, all that success can take on a different meaning now. As one woman told me: "If I hadn't waited so long, if I hadn't been trying to have it all, I would probably be a mother now. At first, when I didn't conceive, I was really kind of relieved. I didn't know if I was ready to be a mother. My career had always come first; how was I going to make that change in myself? But when a year came around and still nothing had happened, relief turned to panic, and panic completely overtook any worries I'd had about being ready. What if I never got pregnant? Was I going to be punished for putting it off so long? Did I have to pay the price for trying to be more than my mother had been—for trying to be more than just-a-mom?"

For as much as we can feel ourselves to be liberated, when something goes wrong we invoke supernatural explanations, if not notions of downright divine punishment and retribution for sin. The contemporary woman is no more prone to be rational in her explanations of her shattering infertility than her grandmother might have been. Despite all of our scientific knowledge, the whole business of creating babies is still quite magical in our minds.

Some women even blame themselves for the ambivalence that led them to postpone motherhood, seeing that ambivalence as a direct cause of their fertility problem. A woman might imagine that her body suppressed its reproductive functions because, secretly, her ambivalent mind was telling it to. So her infertility was entirely "her fault." We really can be so harsh on ourselves!

Besides being a way of explaining infertility, self-blame can also represent an unconscious way of staying stuck and not dealing with the task of choosing. Blaming yourself will certainly not help you move forward. It is more useful to look at what brought you to this point. Why was choosing so hard? Why did you avoid it? Why did you postpone? As you address these questions, respect that there were good psychological reasons why you could not deal with these issues before. Our culture's message, "Develop yourself first: there's no rush!" provided you with the perfect rationale for not dealing earlier with your mixed feelings about motherhood.

BACK ON THE PENDULUM

After the jolt of not conceiving "naturally," many women find themselves questioning why they really want a child. As a woman I interviewed said, "I think the longer you wait, the bigger the issues become about parenting. About why you even want children. And the older you get and the more difficult it becomes physically, you start to think, 'Is it pure vanity wanting children? What do I want kids for?'"

She continued: "The *really* big question is, in terms of not having children, what is the meaning of life? I've always figured that children were the natural answer to the meaning of life; you didn't really have to think about it. You are here to put children on the earth and they are going to be what you leave behind. And since I don't believe in any kind of afterlife, it's particularly depressing to me to think that nobody's going to remember whether I was here or not. And so on the one hand you think that's why women naturally have kids, to take away the pressure of those kinds of thoughts; on the other hand maybe children are just a crutch."

Once this woman decided to become a mother in some other way, she had to go on a campaign. For her to really devote herself to this campaign, she had to suppress her conflicts around motherhood so she could sustain her motivation through what she had to endure. She had to become unequivocal in her desire for a child as she began to undergo fertility treatments. She felt she could no longer ask herself why she wanted children.

Another woman, during seven years of trying various routes to motherhood, buried her terror about replicating her own mother's mothering. Once deciding to take the plunge and have a baby, she had entered therapy to work on this fear. The work stopped when she realized she had a serious fertility problem. When she finally heard that she was to become an adoptive mother in a week, she panicked. Once again the old terror engulfed her and she reentered therapy.

It is not just that an infertile woman has to devote all her energies to becoming a mother. It is also that each failure to become a mother tends to make her more keenly aware of her desire for a child and less conscious of the factors that made her uneasy about motherhood. Whether an expected adoption failed to materialize or a high-tech procedure failed to result in conception, she can experience the depression that accompanies any kind of unfulfilled promise. But when success is finally on the doorstep, her uneasiness or ambivalence may return.

There have been cases of women becoming pregnant through assisted conception and terminating their hard-won pregnancies for all the reasons that made defining themselves as mothers so difficult in the first place. When being a mother is finally on the doorstep, no longer a fantasy, the negative valence of some earlier ambivalence can take over and be very frightening.

That is why I urge the woman who decides, with some mixed feelings, to become a mother not to be ashamed of ambivalence or to suppress it, to stop along the way and once more listen to the conflicting voices within herself—voices about the body, about the role of mother, about being a "normal" woman—and once more see where the balance falls.

As one woman told me, "Infertility slows down the process of becoming a mother. It gave me time to do a lot of work around my own childhood, to become a better mother to myself. I would not have been able to do all this in nine months." The more a woman is able to deal with her issues around mothering during the extended waiting period that infertility often amounts to, the more comfortably she will be able to sit with what happens in the end—whether she chooses to persevere or not.

If she sustains her decision to go ahead with her campaign, her choices are defined by the absence or presence of biological bonds between one or both parents and the child. She has to distinguish between wanting to "have a baby" and wanting to mother a child.

MAKING CHOICES: DEFINING YOURSELF AGAIN

The infertile woman has to decide among four routes available to her. She can choose to be rendered fertile through one or more methods of assisted reproduction. These procedures, most commonly in vitro fertilization and gamete interfallopian transfer, are costly, time consuming, painful, emotionally and physically exhausting—and the chances of success are not high.

If she cannot carry a baby or she decides to give up on the high-tech route, she can opt for surrogacy, in which case she will have neither the physical experiences of pregnancy and birth nor a genetic link to her child. But her partner will be its genetic father.

She can decide to adopt, in which case neither she nor her partner will be biological parents.

Or she can choose to give up trying to become a mother to a child of her own. This can be a difficult adjustment for a woman who has envisioned herself as someday being a traditional mother, especially given the promise of biological motherhood held out by the infertility experts.

The Biological Route

Loudly trumpeted by the media, the new technologies of assisted conception have become an apple too tempting to resist. In fact, 85 percent, on the average, of in vitro procedures are unsuccessful, though this figure is decreasing. Nevertheless, most women begin this voyage assuming, and being urged by the medical profession to believe, that they will be among the 15 percent of those successful.

As soon as a woman even suspects fertility problems, she begins to look to the apple for redemption. How can she not bite, once at least, when it offers so much? Unless the cost of assisted reproductive technology seems prohibitive, the knowledge that it is available has to color your thinking about your infertility.

"I figured, well, if we can't have a baby this way, we'll do it another way," my friend Penny told me. "The in vitro will work. Even if we had been told there was only one chance in a hundred that it would work, my feeling was, if someone has to be the one in a hundredth couple, why not us? I was a different person then. I was much more optimistic."

Penny had struggled with her initial feelings of anger and betrayal when she was diagnosed with blocked fallopian tubes. She had undergone major surgery to correct the problem—unsuccessfully. And now she was looking to the next stage. For her, this meant exploring the possibilities of in vitro fertilization, in which eggs are removed surgically or transvaginally, fertilized with sperm, and placed in the uterus. To prepare her body for this procedure, a woman must first administer herself a course of daily hormonal therapy so that her body will be maximally receptive. Meanwhile, she must be monitored by ultrasound and blood hormone tests.

"Besides the pain," Penny said, "the expenditure of time, money, and energy, the sheer physical strain of it all, I felt humiliated and invaded. It was as if my body were no longer my own. I felt I had no control whatsoever; the doctors were in charge. And the more new and exciting the technology and the procedure, the more likely you are to be talking to a medical technocrat whose interest is in the procedure. They're not necessarily interested in you as a person."

Why would a woman decide to put herself through this procedure several times despite everything it costs her emotionally, physically, and financially?

Some women seek, through a biological connection to the child, some kind of continuity of genetics and of tradition—the family nose, certain mannerisms, the pregnancy lore passed down from generation to generation. Others feel that they will be able to experience themselves as real women only through their pregnant and birthing bodies. One woman I spoke with explained it by saying: "Women who have children and don't have children, there is a difference between them in terms of animalism. Giving birth is a very animalistic thing to go through. When you don't go through it, you are in a way more separated from nature. There's a little detachment there." For her, being separated from nature meant being less womanly.

Penny was not desperate to "clone" herself. It mattered very little to her that her child resemble her physically or temperamentally. Neither did she care about passing on her genes: "There are a lot of myths about that—like, we assume that if we had a biological baby it would be born brilliant. But I'm not a genetic gem." And she had never felt that she would not be a real woman if she couldn't give birth to a child. "My sense of being a woman is not tied up in my reproductive organs. My sense of being a woman is tied up in my capacity to respond to men, and to get a response from them. But I felt great inadequacy and sadness about depriving my husband of something. I felt a lot of grief around that."

For Penny the desire to become a mother was intricately linked with her relationship with her husband. She would have been perfectly happy to have an adopted baby to mother. But he wanted a biological child. On a level of loving connectedness, she wanted to give her husband *his* child.

There was also something in the shared joy of pregnancy and birth to which Penny had really been looking forward. "I would like to put his head on my belly and let him feel the baby kick; I would like to give birth with my husband there to share the experience."

Besides, Penny told me, when she started on the biological route she had no idea what she was in for. By the time she did know, the pregnancy always seemed to be just around the corner. How could she give up now?

In Vitro: The Pendulum Suspended

By the time Penny was resigning herself to the probability that she would never be able to give birth to a biological child, she had undergone six in vitros—three with her own eggs, three with a donor's. Each time, she had been subjected to general anesthesia and had lost and gained many pounds from stress. She had approached this campaign in much the same way that she had approached other challenges in her accomplished life—with determination, efficiency, and a sense that nothing is impossible for a woman today. Each time she failed, this feeling about herself and the world was dashed. For Penny, such an erosion of confidence—a confidence that had been handed down by her father, an immigrant who made good—was in itself a significant loss.

"My whole sense that things turn out okay in the end if you just keep trying," she said, "my sense that hard work can do it, you just have to work hard enough and study hard enough, my sense of the world as a manageable place where effort pays off—I don't have that sense any more. And that feels sad."

For a long time Penny's optimism and her sense that nothing was impossible had been fed by the enthusiastic optimism of the fertility specialists, who seemed drunk on the ever-expanding possibilities of the new technologies. It was their cheerleading encouragement, their "you only fail when you stop trying," that had made it so difficult for Penny to stop taking bites of the apple. Penny had been educated for success. How could she become a quitter?

The Addiction to High Tech's Promise

I spoke with a psychotherapist specializing in fertility issues, Dee Paddock, about this syndrome that is so common among women engaged in assisted reproductive procedures. She described it in a personal communication (1994) as feeling, for many women, like an addiction. I find this a useful framework for understanding the experience of a woman who endures years of turmoil in her efforts to conceive a biological child—even though she knows that what she is doing contradicts her own definition of reasonable and healthy behavior.

Using a formal model of substance addiction, Paddock describes the real loss of power that an infertile woman experiences during the high-tech process, combined with an illusion of being in control—"I can stop any time"—at the same time as "I can make this happen."

The need to maintain this illusion can result in several tendencies: a woman becomes increasingly compulsive and obsessive in her attempt to conceive; she develops a pattern of living from cycle to cycle, from "fix" to "fix," as a way of evoking a sense of progress and avoiding the pain of knowing that she cannot be in control of her body; she becomes crisis oriented, involved in every detail of her treatment in order to feel that she is playing an active role; she begins to feel as if the world revolves around her problem; she lives only for herself, for her next treatment, and between treatments can feel nothing but the emptiness within her.

The idea of quitting can be more terrifying than any of the horrors of treatment. As long as a woman keeps trying, she can shield herself from the term *infertile* and from the sense of helplessness infertility creates. At the same time, as Penny's story shows, each unsuccessful attempt erodes a woman's faith in her ability to manage, her confidence that she can control her own fate. She lives with this conflict, unable to tell herself to stop trying and yet dreading the next procedure even while she hopes it may be *the* one.

Ultimately, Penny had to tell herself that enough was enough. Statistics that once had told her she had a 15 percent chance of conceiving now seemed to be saying she had an 85 percent chance of *not* conceiving. Now she and her husband were faced with the choice of where to go from here. Penny was ready—had been ready for quite some time—to go ahead and try to adopt. Although her husband still had his hopes pinned on a child of his own, he agreed to try adoption. And in the meantime Penny agreed to look into the possibility of surrogacy.

The Surrogacy Route

Penny had assumed, as do many who are opposed to surrogacy, that a woman automatically feels bonded as a mother to the child she is carrying; it is part of the mythology of "natural" womanhood. How can she bear to give up her baby? How can she be required to, should she change her mind?

"I felt totally negative about it," Penny told me. "I had this stereotypic model of poor women being exploited by upper-middle-class couples who were buying babies. It felt very wrong to me."

Penny's experience led her to question the stereotype of the "poor and exploited surrogate mother." She began to see that a woman might have good reasons to use her body in the service of another's needs.

"My feelings about surrogacy changed when I met two surrogate moms who blew me away. They were totally different from what I had expected. They were both educated, interesting, and incredibly generous. Neither was doing it for money.

"I hadn't been able to imagine what kind of woman could give up the child she had carried. I still don't understand it in terms of my experience of trying for so long to conceive. But both these women were very clear that from the beginning they didn't feel the child was theirs. It was a child they were helping to create as a gift to someone infertile."

The two candidates for surrogacy whom Penny met may not be representative of surrogate mothers as a group; nevertheless, as examples they show us that generalizations about surrogacy can be misleading. And they provide examples of women who, because they do not entertain fantasies of nurturing the babies they bear, do not define themselves as these children's mothers.

It is desire, intention, and ultimately a conscious self-definition that makes a woman a mother; it is the meaning that each pregnancy, each attempt to conceive, each attempt to adopt, has for her. We recognize this interpretation of parenthood when we agree that a male sperm donor may not be the father of the child, though he is the progenitor.

Each of the surrogates Penny met with had children of her own; they were both clear that they did not want more. One of them had a good job as an accountant and a daughter and husband both of whom she described as "wonderful." Completely satisfied with her life, she said she wanted to do "something extraordinary." The second woman Penny interviewed had once erroneously been told she could not have children, and had been forced to deal with how devastating that felt. She had not given up trying, though, and now had two sons. When Penny met her, she had already been through three surrogate pregnancies. Her motivation was clear: she really felt a deep empathy for infertile women. She wanted to give them the babies they so desired just as she had experienced her own children as gifts to her.

Although Penny's conceptualization of surrogacy was altered through her meetings with potential surrogates, she remained wary. "There's a lot that can go wrong. And given all that we've been through, I don't know if I could handle any more complications."

While Penny and her husband continued to consider the option of surrogacy, an adoption agency they had contacted about a year earlier called to announce that a baby would be available within a week.

After all they had been through, they finally became parents.

The Adoption Route

Since abortions have become more readily available and single mothering by choice more acceptable, the number of healthy adoptable infants has dropped to an all-time low. This poses a real question for the prospective adoptive mother: How long am I prepared to wait? Am I prepared to adopt an older child? A disabled child? One of the kids that get left behind?

Penny came to adoption as a final choice, and only after she was finally able to say "no" to any more attempts at in vitro fertilization. Had she been as adverse to the notion of parenting a nonbiological child as her husband was, they might have chosen to remain childless. Had Penny not been so clear about wanting to become a mother, she might have been less prepared to embark on yet another emotionally exhausting roller coaster.

Penny was lucky to finally be offered an adoptive child. Many would-be parents have grown reluctant to adopt in light of the heartbreaking custody battles that have hit the media in recent years. While these stories are not representative of the typical adoption experience, their sensational details have been frightening to both prospective and actual adoptive parents. One woman, who had been raising her 5-year-old adopted daughter almost since birth, told me, "I still get upset when I hear about these legal battles. It scares me that at any time, someone could come out of the blue and take my baby away."

A couple considering adoption might also be concerned about having no control over the child's congenital predispositions. You might wonder: How different from myself and my partner might this child be in endowment? How different from its other adopted siblings? You might wonder about prenatal influences or about inherited illnesses and disabilities. Of course, we can just as easily be faced with these potential problems in our own biological children as in an adopted child.

For all these reasons—biology, emotional exhaustion, anxiety, and, of course, legal and ethical issues—adoption does feel like a poor last resort to many women (although you might choose adoption over the biological route if the physical realities of pregnancy and birth don't appeal to you).

Says Dee Paddock (1994): "We bang our heads against the wall because when we walk into the adoption agency we feel as if we're backtracking. There's a tendency to feel, 'I'm doing worse than I was before; here I am at the adoption agency and I'm really thinking I'd like to try one more in vitro.' It feels like regression."

The Adoption Pendulum

I described earlier how the woman attempting to conceive through high-tech procedures can easily become trapped in a trying game. This does not end when she turns to adoption as a last resort. It is a different kind of emotional roller coaster. You still ask yourself, when is enough enough? How many failed placements? How many agencies? How many birth-mother-match meetings? How many social workers coming into your home to conduct home studies? If you judged yourself—your ambivalence, your liberated past— when you first discovered your infertility, how will it feel to have somebody come into your life and judge you?

We assume that once a woman decides to try for adoption she has given up on the idea of conceiving a biological child. It's a false assumption. That feeling of "maybe next time" may still govern. The doctor's office, with its wall of baby pictures, still beckons. One woman told me that even after becoming a mother to three adopted children, she *still* thought about resuming fertility treatment and trying for a biological child.

"A woman going this route," said Paddock (1994), "has to learn to live with a fairly high level of ambivalence. But I think that we grow in our whole experience of being by becoming better able to deal with the gray." As I've said before, life is about living with conflict.

There is a tendency for a woman becoming an adoptive mother to try and bury the grief she still feels about her inability to have a biological child. Not only does the grief feel terribly painful to her, she also feels that to be conscious of it would amount to a betrayal of the child she has brought into her home. But, as Penny put it, "One of the things I've been learning about adoption is the grief that we feel about infertility in many ways may mirror the grief the baby will someday most likely feel about the loss of its biological parents. Maybe if we can be straight about our loss in not having the biological child we so wanted, and if we can openly express it, then we can help our adopted child experience their loss."

REDEFINING YOURSELF

Some women cannot consider adopting a child. It might be that the very notion feels too alien. Perhaps it was the "having a baby" more than the mothering itself that felt so important. Or maybe a woman's partner refuses to adopt and she is faced with choosing the partnership over motherhood.

A couple might embark on the adoption process but end up choosing not to continue because they are not prepared to wait for the kind of child they want. A woman who is clear that she cannot or will not accept a handicapped baby, an older child, or an infant who is not racially matched to herself and her partner might want to look at why she feels this way and whether she can feel differently, or redefine herself as a woman who will not mother.

What then?

She can become childless.

Or she can become childfree.

By *childfree* I mean that instead of defining yourself as a woman who was cheated of motherhood, you define yourself as someone who has chosen a life without children as being more in keeping with a sense of yourself as a person than are the mothering options remaining to you. Ultimately, a woman's response to her infertility depends on her fantasy of fulfillment and how fixed that fantasy is for her. Generativity and creativity can have many expressions.

In her autobiography, Margaret Mead (1972) tells the story of how, at the age of 25, she was told by her doctor that she would probably never be able to have children because of a tipped uterus. She had always imagined being a mother to a horde of kids—and as the wife of a minister had fantasized about settling down with him to start her family in some country parish.

When it became apparent that her fantasy was not going to materialize because she was infertile, she readjusted her vision of her future life. She had fallen in love with a fellow social scientist during her first marriage. As long as she still saw herself as a future mother she decided not to follow her heart but to stay with her husband who, she felt, would make a wonderful father. Now, with motherhood apparently out of the question for her, she decided to divorce and marry the man with whom she could envision sharing a life of fieldwork and intellectual endeavor. The fact that she did *not* see him as the kind of father she would want for her children was not particularly relevant.

Though Mead secretly harbored the hope that someday her doctor might be proved wrong, she nevertheless clearly redefined herself as a woman who would not mother. "Something very special sometimes happens to women when they know they will not have a child—or any more children," she wrote in her autobiography (1972), basing her generalization on her own response. ". . . Suddenly their whole creativity is released. They write or paint as never before or they throw themselves into academic work with enthusiasm, where before they had only half a mind to spare for it" (p. 246).

No longer bound by the stricture that prevented women in their reproductive years from undertaking fieldwork in remote places, she made it known that she could be sent anywhere a man would be sent.

I believe Mead was able to redefine the nature of herself as a generative person—a person whose life would be fertile despite the absence of motherhood—in part because her work was so fulfilling. Also, she had been raised in a family, atypical in those years, that expected women to lead intellectual lives and to be responsible and active citizens of their world.

In addition, Mead was relatively young when she found that she might never be a mother. Though she had a notion of having it all in her future, at the age of 25 she was still focused on the nonmothering part of "all." When motherhood came as a surprise at the age of 38, she was thrilled. Once again, she was able to transform herself in light of the vicissitudes of her life with great creative energy, shaping a motherhood that was entirely her own. It was her creativity, as a mother and otherwise, that made Mead feel at one with herself.

Becoming Childfree

In their book *Sweet Grapes* (1989), Jean and Michael Carter describe how they transformed their definitions of themselves from being childless to being childfree. They had struggled with the wrenching reality of infertility. They had contended with repeated failures on the high-tech route. They had mourned the loss of the children they thought they would have and the parents they thought they would be. Finally they decided that they would be happiest if they could stop experiencing themselves as lacking and capitalize on their gains instead. That meant giving up their campaign to have a baby.

What was there in their lives as nonparents that helped them feel good about themselves, they wondered? What experiences had they found gratifying despite the fact that they had no children?

The Carters were lucky enough to have absorbing and fulfilling careers; he was an English professor, she was a gynecologist-obstetrician. As a childless couple they could really immerse themselves in their work. Delivering babies, of course, had been a heartbreaking occupation for an infertile woman. But as she evolved into someone who no longer defined herself as infertile she learned that it did not have to be so painful.

Having made their decision, the Carters were deliberate and unsentimental in their reorientation. They write:

"The future nursery turned into a music room. The dolls we had been saving for our daughters were set aside for our nieces. The money we had been putting away as a college fund became our opportunity to travel. After dozens of these little transformations, we realized that we had made a major change in our lives. Instead of being unsuccessful parents-to-be, we were very successful non-parents" (p. 27).

The real punch line in Jean Carter's evolution to a truly childfree state was delivered when she came home one day bearing a package of contraceptive sponges. "Contraception was our declaration of independence from the cycle of hope and despair" (p. 27). She had reached the point where she could feel in control over her body. Fully aware that her relationship with her body was a part of her self-definition, she was ultimately defining herself as a woman who had chosen not to be a mother.

7

On the Other Side
of Choosing:
Life as a Mother

*T*his chapter and the next look at how the experiences of being a mother and not mothering—and especially the response to the various emotional challenges of each route—are shaped to a large extent by the journeys women have made to get there, whether their choices were passive or active ones, and the extent to which they were able to accept and understand their many feelings.

The stories you will read here are based on the experiences of patients and on interviews I conducted with women who are mothers and women who are living lives without children. You might be tempted to look at other women's stories and imagine that those stories will become your own. To the extent that every woman's story is unique, I offer little comfort that this will be so. On the other hand, perhaps the stories of others will resonate for you. One thing that is fairly universal: the struggle for self-understanding and self-acceptance does not end when we reach the other side of the journey toward a decision.

One of the most powerful fears in choosing to mother or not to mother is the fear of loss. If I don't become a mother, will I miss a special connection to another person? Will I miss being the mother some part of me thought I'd become? And in the face of censure, will I lose my sense of belonging? If I do have a child, will I lose my independent self, the me who makes strides in the world, the me who feels competent in the things I undertake?

My sample reflects the fact that in our society women without children are far more comfortable than women who are mothers in expressing regrets. Women who have deeply regretted becoming mothers do not reveal themselves easily. I have found that for a woman to talk about that experience feels to her like a shameful confession and a rejection of the child whom she may love very much.

One woman who heard me arranging an interview with a woman who had had fertility problems, piped up: "Do you want to interview any women who regret having kids?"

"Yes, indeed," I replied enthusiastically, and made an appointment back-to-back with the first woman, who was her friend. It seemed to me that she was eager to be finally able to talk. When the day of the interview arrived, however, her friend told me that she had canceled, that she was just too embarrassed to talk about her regrets.

I tried using the Internet to find women who regretted having children because I thought the impersonal nature of the Net would encourage some honest responses. Although women were forthcoming about many other motherhood experiences, not one mother addressed the issue of regret.

The fact is, whichever route a woman takes, she loses something. One of the things I hope the stories in these chapters will reflect is that when a woman makes a choice based on a thoughtful exploration of all her voices, she does not lose her self in any permanent way. Ultimately, whatever choice she makes, *she will find that she is still herself, and more,* more because she will have gained a truly mature sense of who she is. Whatever she loses— independence, connection to a child—she will likely fill the space left with something that is meaningful to her.

That does not mean that, having crossed to the other side, she will be impervious to others' criticism of her or to the ambivalence that will well up in her. She might not be the ever-loving, selfless mother of her fantasies; she might occasionally regret having never done what most women do. But it should not feel so difficult, because hopefully she will have developed the tools to help her understand why she struck her particular bargain, and to deal with the voices that are causing static in her life.

MOTHERHOOD: A VARIABLE EXPERIENCE

The experience of motherhood is infinitely variable. It depends on many factors, some of which are in constant flux: who you are, who your child is, the social and familial context in which you mother, the circumstances of your life, your choices as a mother, and how all of these factors meld together. The experience is influenced too by your fantasy of motherhood, how fixed that fantasy is, and the degree to which it reflects what you really experience.

A woman who has really explored herself and thought clearly about her choice to mother has an understanding of some of these variables, specifically, those connected with who she is. However ambivalent she has been about becoming a mother, understanding herself makes a difference in how she adjusts to what cannot be anticipated in life, in particular, the nature of the child and the vicissitudes of the child's development. Moreover, having explored the aspects of becoming a mother that most trouble her, and having accepted her mixed feelings, she is better equipped to cope with the almost inevitable surprises, changes, and ambivalence she will undoubtedly experience as a mother.

What is constant and predictable is that there will be frequent changes affecting every woman's experience of parenthood.

Experience and Fantasy: The Unanticipated

No woman can really know what motherhood will be like for her. Even women who are clear about wanting to have babies and care for them have moments when their experiences do not match their fantasies; this may make them feel less than their whole selves as mothers, women, or persons. Especially if they hold to a notion of how motherhood *should* be and feel, certain circumstances may lead them to feel mystified, if not deeply troubled, that their experience is not what it was supposed to be.

Who the Child Is

The real baby is rarely the one you imagine in your mind's eye before you first meet it. From the very beginning of your lives together, you are faced with the task of reconciling your fantasy with the real baby before you.

If you have fantasized about holding a constantly smiling, cute baby, and now you have a baby who is neither cute nor smiley, how do you cope?

In my experience, the women who cope best have become aware of their fantasies such that they can contrast and reconcile the fantasy against the reality of who the child is. As I see it, parents' main responsibility is to know their child.

If I contributed to my daughter's sanity in any way, the magic moment came, I believe, when she was about 2 years old. She was getting out of the car very, very slowly, and at first I thought, Oh my God, I've got a passive-aggressive child! Suddenly I was struck with the blessed insight that her tempo, constitutionally given, was different from mine. She was getting out of the car so slowly because she did things more slowly than I did. I had to realize that *I* tend to move very fast; *she* tends to be pretty normal in her movements.

There are, certainly, children who, given who they are, can make mothering more fraught with problems. Your child might be one who is difficult to parent, perhaps a child with a physical or mental disability. Or it might be a fussy baby, a colicky baby, an irritable baby, a baby who does not like to be cuddled because it is hyper-

sensitive to touch. You could end up with a child whose tempera-
ment, diametrically opposed to your own, makes the job of parenting
seem terribly hard and unrewarding. A mother's struggles around
such a child, her constant mystification, can make her feel incompetent, and that sense of herself as an incompetent mother can make
her feel miserable about the job she has chosen to do—like a failed
mother.

Changing Life Circumstances

Just as we cannot know in advance who our child will be, we cannot anticipate changes in our life circumstances. You might be
distressed to find the relationship with your partner diminish-
ing as you both focus your attentions on a child. You might find
yourself at some point in your child's life parenting alone and
completely unprepared for the multiple roles involved in paying
the bills and raising a child. Accidents, illness, death, economic
reversal—all of these can alter the experience of parenting.

Gena's Story

The story of Gena demonstrates why it is important to understand
the fantasies that have contributed to your wanting to become a
mother. Gena had grown up as the daughter of an utterly detached
mother and a father who, though loving, was alcoholic and vola-
tile. Motherhood, for her, was in part a means of fulfilling her
fantasy of having a normal family of her own, in part her desire to
repair the damaging parenting she had received and repeat the
nurturant mothering that had been provided her by a wonderful
neighbor—a very maternal woman who probably saved her psychic
life.

Having spent years in therapy before I interviewed her, Gena
was fully aware of this reparative need and had identified her fan-

tasies with regard to mothering; in the beginning she found those fantasies fulfilled. She told me: "I just thought I had died and gone to heaven! In my fantasies I had imagined making homemade food—which I actually did for a while. I had imagined breast feeding—which I actually did. And being a mother connected me with the world. I would walk down the street with my baby and everybody would stop and talk to me."

Then Gena's husband died. She found herself parenting a 7-year-old daughter in a diminished family of two, in a community where the norm was mom, dad, and two kids. The context for her mothering no longer matched her fantasy of family life. Yet, because she had come to mothering with a good understanding of all that it represented for her, she was able to cope with the devastation of her loss of family by retaining a meaningful sense of what kind of a mother she could still be.

The Developing Child

Life is a videotape, not a snapshot; it keeps moving and changing. In no area of life is this more true than in parenting; the job requirements, its benefits, and its stresses all keep changing from the moment of first holding your infant to the time when that child is ready to live as an adult. When a woman becomes a mother, she will be most stable if she is prepared for the continual changes that occur around a developing child—even the most unpredictable shifts—and for the fact that some stages will feel more comfortable, given who she is.

Some women feel more comfortable in the relationship to their children as their role becomes less one of custodial nurturer and more one of a fun-loving Brownie leader. Others find that they feel most fulfilled taking care of infants. I was told about a woman who sought therapy for a deep depression that had hit her at the same time that she bought her baby his first-ever pair of shoes; the shoes, she realized in treatment, represented her child's first step toward independence, his ability to walk away from her and begin to shape a life of his own experiences, without her.

Anticipating Ambivalence

Although you cannot know for sure how you will feel as a mother or how that feeling might change over time, you can anticipate some of the negative or ambivalent feelings you might experience around motherhood, given a good measure of self-awareness and a realistic appraisal of what mothering is. It is certainly not uncommon for women today to experience a yearning for more time, more independence; a sense of nostalgia for that old, preparent self; feelings of entrapment; feelings of resentment toward this utterly dependent creature; a nagging sense of discomfort in the maternal role. These sensations can make you feel both nostalgic for your old self and intensely guilty.

Nevertheless, many women find in motherhood something positive for themselves that far outweighs the negatives. I remember hearing Toni Morrison speak in 1993 about her experience as a mother. She recalled the physical exhaustion, the curtailment of freedom that being a mother entailed—and the sense of liberation that her relationship with her children provided her. With them she did not have to be the novelist, the university professor, the public speaker, all the roles people wanted her to play. Her children, she said, needed only to have her be herself.

Like many women, Jean—my art-dealer patient who introduced me to the idea of the "pendulum"—had worried about losing herself in motherhood. When I later asked her whether, as the mother of a 2-year-old, her fears had come true, she told me: "I am the same person I was. I didn't really give up any part of me; the difficulty is integrating the two. To counteract the risk of losing myself I have actively focused on doing things that just have to do with me; for example, I took up dance classes again."

There was a history of postpartum depression in Jean's family, a history she had been terrified of repeating: How had she fared after the birth of her baby? "I was afraid I would have it, and I did. But I don't have it any more. I was on the lookout for it; I got treatment early and tackled it aggressively.

"I was also worried about the impact a baby would have on my marriage, and I was right to be. In some ways we're closer and in some ways we're not. But it'll change. When the baby's older and the focus is not on him so much, there'll be more room in the relationship for us.

"One of the things I really worried about was my work and that seems very trivial now, because the baby seems so much more important than my work. I just adore him.

"So, yes, having a child has gotten in the way of my relationship to my husband, myself, my work. The kid has become the first priority. But with all the conflicts, if you're able to manage these issues of motherhood there's nothing more gratifying. And you know, the child feels conflict too. One minute he wants me to take care of him, the next minute he wants to be independent."

Giving Yourself Wide Margins

A woman who can adjust to the inevitable shifts in her life, knowing that they are time limited, can more readily accept her ambivalence about mothering. She can enjoy the good and take the bad with a philosophical shrug—and reorganize her life in such a way as to stay balanced. It is not always easy to remember that difficult times will pass; talking to other parents and friends who have been through similar stages in their children's lives can be a very supportive experience.

The point is to know your vulnerabilities and, to the extent that you cannot adjust your mothering to suit you, to give yourself latitude for ambivalence as well as leeway for less-than-perfect mothering—something Stephanie, a woman who "occasionally regrets" becoming a mother, failed to do. She defined *motherly* as being a constantly present caregiver, but full-time caregiving did not suit her. Had she had a more flexible definition, she could have arranged her life in a way that would have made sense for who she was—or at least forgiven herself for hating it when she was stuck caring for her child and simply let herself complain about a "mommy jail."

Stephanie told me: "Before I had Melissa I had never taken care of anyone in my life, except myself. I assumed the maternal thing would just come out of having a baby. I never thought it would make me feel so out of whack.

"The first few months were terrible. I think I loved the baby. But I hated feeling tied to her, dealing with her as a constant presence. I couldn't afford baby-sitters, and my husband thought it was my job—like, I was better at it because I was the mommy. I guess I thought I should be, too.

"It got easier to enjoy her as she got older and less bound to me. But to this day—she's 8 now—I get in a rotten mood whenever she's sick. I dread having to be really motherly. I find myself resenting her for putting me in that position. I think if I'd had a child who was sick a lot, or who was emotionally needy, I would have been a miserable mother."

Another woman, Joy, who was perfectly comfortable being the full-time nurturer of her child, told a different story. "I love changing the diapers, I love holding her all the time, I love comforting her when she's sick or upset. That's what a parent does. I love being her mommy." Joy's difficulties around mothering—what clouded it for her—stemmed from the fact that as a single working mother she was continuously stressed and could not forgive herself. "I tend to fly off the handle," she told me, "and that makes me feel like a terrible mother. It's very painful."

LISTENING TO YOUR VOICES

Any choice about motherhood—even after one has defined oneself as a woman who will have children—entails some degree of separation from one's own past voices and an effort to create a new mothering person.

When you listen to all the voices that are telling you what you are supposed to be doing and feeling as a mother, remember: *some of these old, internalized voices lie.*

I remember once, before I became a mother, the comment a man made as he saw me carrying a friend's infant. "You look wonderful holding a baby!" he said. I might have been taken in by his vision of me as a blissful Madonna with child—a vision rooted in the stereotype of blissful mother–infant symbiosis. Had I been—had his comment played any part in my choice to become a mother—I would have been wholly unprepared for the reality of mothering. I would have been unable to accept that, for me, mothering could be wonderfully fulfilling as long as I could find a little time for myself during the day.

It is a matter of sorting out the purely romantic representations of motherhood from the images that resonate with some sense of what could be real. It is not an easy discrimination. But having made it, you can then try to separate out the images that ring true *for you* from those that could never fit. You can ready yourself for the possibility that you will have a child who you have wanted very much, yet who is capable of making you feel at times raging, resentful, unmotherly—of shattering your image of yourself as the eternally "good mother."

You can also prepare yourself for the possibility that, though you had always imagined yourself returning quite happily to your work within a few weeks of the birth, when the time comes you might be scarcely able to bear leaving your baby. As Margaret Mead, according to her daughter (Bateson 1989), commented in connection with the problem some mothers have of sustaining a commitment to work: it's not that the baby cries so much, it's that the baby smiles so much.

Having It All

We are urged, as modern women, to believe that we should have fulfilling careers, be fabulous mothers, and enjoy the most gratifying of marriages. Most women pay dearly for trying to fulfill these expectations. The conflict between work and mothering is one that is likely to be encountered by any woman who has internalized traditional expectations of motherhood and its joys, yet whose sense of herself and her potential have also been shaped by contemporary voices and norms—in short, who brings her mother's voice into a world of complex and shifting expectations regarding what women can and should do.

For the contemporary woman, being "just-a-mother" can feel as socially unacceptable as being childfree. Both are outside the scope of what we are supposed to be. Many women feel guilty about their choice to leave the workforce and become full-time mothers.

"People ask me what I do," one woman told me in an interview, "and when I tell them I'm a homemaker they look upon me in a certain way. It's not particularly nice. It's dismissive. Luckily I live in an artistic community where the idea of people doing something important to them that they don't get paid a dime for is pretty common. But especially in circles where there are more career women, I feel I'm perceived as less of a person to be considered. People assume a kind of brain deadness about mothering. How could anyone interesting do only that? And then if I say, 'Well, I've been working on some writing,' they want to know all about it."

The alternative to full-time mothering—having it all—is no easier. A good friend of mine, the very involved mother of three young children, expressed to me how much stress she experiences juggling all the other things she does—from her professional work as a clinical psychologist to her active participation on special PTA committees; from several hours of gratifying volunteer work in a woman's shelter to running a household. Although she has chosen to do every one of these things and would not give them up for anything, she feels her life is teetering on the edge of a precipice and that, were she to shift even slightly in how she has arranged it all, the whole thing would come tumbling down—despite an egalitarian marriage and baby-sitters.

Since Arlie Hochschild published *Second Shift* in 1989, several studies have confirmed that, however deeply the father is involved in parenting, it is generally the mother who takes up the slack domestically. She works full time and comes home to a second shift. She also bears the responsibility of keeping track—food that needs to be bought, homework that has to be done, play dates that have to be organized, calls to the baby-sitter, sick days. She is the Central Committee. Certainly, a few women are able to quite comfortably let their partners take care of everything domestic and maternal. It is harder for a woman who hears the voice of her own mother telling her, "However tedious the day-to-day stuff of mothering might be, it's the bedrock of the mother–child relationship."

One woman I interviewed told me how, when her first child was born, her husband was unemployed while she was doing well as an executive editor in a publishing company. So she continued to work, and her husband stayed home with the baby. "He had no conception that he was going to bond with the kid like this, and he bonded so tight and so hard that he wouldn't let go. He was doing everything for her. So I would come home from work and have to stand in line for my baby. I felt a real longing, a real lack of fulfillment with this child. I really had wanted a baby, and now I had one, and I had to stand in line to get to her. I felt guilty and I felt angry, because this wasn't what my husband was supposed to be doing, and he was good at it."

Even the fact that she is working while her child is being cared for by a sitter can tear at a woman. "My mother always encouraged me to work, but *she* had stayed home," Betsy, a social worker and mother of two, told me. "So I felt like I had no track to step in. I was working two days a week and feeling awful about leaving my children. But I was still doing it, with all that anxiety and all that regret, and never feeling right about it."

Betsy's struggles were centered around the tension she experienced between two voices that created a mixed message: the voice that long ago, in her childhood, had defined *mother* as someone who is always there with and for her kids, and the current one that said she should continue to work, even though she had two small children at home. Both of these voices were her mother's. The earlier one had laid the tracks into which Betsy saw herself stepping. The later one—whether through a sense of regret over her own life or a recognition of changing times—wanted her daughter to pursue her career. "She tried to help me with my anxiety about abandoning my kids. But it just made me feel that maybe my mom wasn't such a hot mother if she could feel comfortable about the idea of leaving two little children at home with a nanny. That's not what a mother does."

A "good" mother would not leave her child ten hours a day. She would not yield the responsibility of feeding, washing, and protecting her child—isn't that what mothers do?—to someone else, and then go out again in the evening, just because there's a movie she wants to see.

The "Good Mother" Mandate

Betsy worried that going out to work made her a "bad" mother—but not that bad. Knowing she really wanted to stay home with her kids made her feel better.

What of the woman who feels a tremendous sense of relief when she reenters the world and once again assumes her nonmaternal identity? She might love and miss her child very much, but she feels uneasy, somewhat disconnected from herself, while she is being mommy.

Her feeling of relief might be heavily tinged with guilt. Although we have grown up to believe that a woman should potentiate herself in the world, we have also inherited a vision of "good mother" that is rooted in notions of woman as "naturally" selfless, nurturant, domestically inclined. Despite many studies to the contrary, the voices of contemporary pediatricians such as Penelope Leach (1994), who advocates full-time mothering as the best possible environment for children and therefore—in a grand leap—for the future of society, only add to the guilt many working mothers experience.

A woman who feels guilty leaving her child so she can work will likely feel even more guilty about taking time for herself in order to feel more like a whole person. An ambivalent mother might feel torn between fulfilling these nonmaternal desires and trying to find fulfillment as a mother; she explains her conflict to herself in terms of the child: "If I satisfy my own needs, my child will suffer."

One of my patients, Sylvie, would come to see me filled with remorse and guilt. "I shouldn't have gone to my meeting last night. My son needed me to be home with him," she told me once.

I asked her, "Whose voice is telling you that?"

Gradually we were able to figure out that when Sylvie was most unforgiving of herself, it was her mother's voice she was listening to. She resented the notion that she had internalized her very critical mother's condemnation of whatever she did. I felt that until she could accept the dissonance between her mother's harsh voice and the different realities with which they each had to deal and their different personalities, she could not feel reasonably content with herself as a mother.

Even after she had recognized the voice that told her she was a bad mother, Sylvie had to struggle with it.

"I am always on the cusp of feeling guilty," Sylvie told me a few sessions later. "If I do anything for myself I feel like I'm forgetting my son. Whenever I have the thought, 'He'll be fine,' I feel guilty. And one of the ways I protect myself from the guilt is by limiting myself. I enjoy things less, do fewer things, and feel less vital. I feel emotionally flattened. Ever since I've been a mother, I've stayed away from experiencing my own needs too strongly. And that's not good for me or my child." Indeed.

What Is a "Good" Mother?

We are constrained as mothers by a host of assumptions about the "good" mother. To a large extent these are based on notions of maternal "instinct." The "good" mother feels naturally and un-ambiguously nurturant toward her child; she unreservedly wants and needs close physical contact with her offspring; she feels her baby's pain, has the urge to soothe it as soon as it cries; her heart breaks when it is time to let go and her child finally walks away from her.

We look at mothers in cultures other than our own—mothers who carry their babies on their hips or backs all day and sleep with them at night, mothers who never let an infant cry—and we might romantically imagine them to be more "natural" and "good" than we are. We imagine, because we interpret the meanings of these maternal behaviors according to our own construction of mother-hood—our myths about what motherhood is and should be.

In fact, anthropologists now believe, if a Paleolithic mother gave her infant the breast the moment it whimpered, it might realistically be to guard against the possibility of predators being alerted by the baby's cry; this was something the mother learned. At the other extreme, a hunter–gatherer mother might choose to kill her newborn infant in "the hungry season" in order to be a good mother to her not-yet-weaned baby, who needs all she can provide in breast milk for its continued adequate nourishment.

In our culture, where pure, physical survival is rarely an issue, where couples can plan their families economically, where middle-class parents are presented daily with the results of child research, it seems there are no limits to what a good mother can do. She can involve herself in every aspect of her child's development in order that it become the best and brightest, the happiest, the most well adjusted to society. Or so she believes. The only limit to "good" mothering, then, seems to be a woman's willingness to sacrifice her own needs—for privacy, space, time, material things—in favor of her child's. The more selfless she is, the better a mother she would appear to be.

In real life, most parents struggle to do what is best for their children. Yet the balance between a parent's needs and those of their children is often difficult if not impossible to strike. What is good for a mother is not necessarily good for her child, and vice versa. So she often compromises one way or the other. She makes choices with the constant tension of being damned no matter what. Her child might be best off staying home with a cold, but the mother who stays home with her child might risk losing her job, missing an important meeting, jeopardizing a promotion. So she sends her child to school.

Does this make her a bad mother?

What *is* a good mother?

One woman I spoke with talked about how self-critical she had been as a parent to her children. "My measure of being a good mother was to be calm and anchored, and to be able to be with them and not go nuts." She had to learn that her own needs for adult stimulation, for peace, for something more than her children could offer her, were valid, even though she might choose to take care of the kids first anyway.

The "Good Enough" Mother

During the mid '50s, at a time when women were beating themselves up because they worried that they were not really good mothers, the pediatrician and psychoanalyst D. W. Winnicott (1955) deconstructed the myth of the perfect mother and coined the term *good-enough mothering*.

Winnicott encouraged us to look at parenting in nonabsolute terms and to understand that one can fall short of being the perfect mother without automatically becoming the destructive mother. He also gave validity to the ambivalent feelings so many mothers feel toward their children. Listing the reasons why any normal woman will sometimes reactively hate her child, he wrote in his inimitably humorous British style: "He [the child] is ruthless, treats her as scum, an unpaid servant, a slave. . . . Having got what he wants he throws her away like orange peel. . . . He is suspicious, refuses her good food, and makes her doubt herself, but eats well with his aunt" (cited in First 1994, p. 154).

Winnicott challenged the prevailing, sentimental notion of unconditional mother love and turned it on its head by asking the extent to which a mother can accept her mixed feelings as part of the fact that she has a self independent of the child and its needs. To what extent can she retain her sense of otherness and still feel reassured that she is not damaging her child? Especially for a woman who has very real opposing pulls toward self as mother and self as other, Winnicott's formulation of good-enough parenting helps strike a more comfortable balance.

8

On the Other Side
of Choosing:
Life without Children

What does it feel like, being a woman without children?

As I interviewed women who had chosen not to become mothers and asked them this question, I was not surprised to find that feelings varied widely, ranging from a profound sense of loss to great pleasure in life. The answers confirmed my belief that women's experiences as nonmothers—parallel to the experiences of mothers—depend largely on how they understand the fact that they are childless. Even women who occasionally regret being childless can experience this regret as a devastated "what have I done?" or as an expected consequence of the risk they took.

Some regretful women explained their childlessness to me in terms of "fate," telling me that the men they found themselves attracted to were never parent material, or that their timing was off—they missed the boat. These women had never asked themselves in what sense the course their lives had taken reflected a choice, albeit an unconscious one. Would they have changed those details of their pasts had they known what they now knew? Had circumstances been conducive to becoming a parent, would they have felt clear about making that choice?

As a 45-year-old woman who initially explained her lack of children to me in terms of "timing" later said: "I'm smart enough to know that had I really wanted children, I would have found a husband and I would have had them. I was having a hard enough time taking care of *me*. I don't think I would have been able to take care of a child. I still don't think I could."

CHILDLESSNESS: THE VARIETY
OF EXPERIENCE

A 43-year-old dancer, Gail, told me: "I know I won't have a kid, and it pains me, it causes me a lot of sadness. I think about it all the time. But there's nothing I can do about it."

For a long time Gail had believed she could never be a mother because she felt like a big grouch whenever she was around her husband's children. She was freed of these feelings only when, after reading an Alice Miller book in her late thirties, she realized that her feelings about children were connected with her experience of her mother as cold and unloving.

With this revelation Gail began to feel more relaxed around children and started yearning for a child of her own. But by now she was married to a man who had children from a previous marriage and did not want another. Besides, Gail felt she was too old to embark on a life of parenting; she had "missed the boat." She assumed that had she transcended her hateful feelings around kids earlier, she would have happily become a good mother. And so it was with great unhappiness and some anger that she resigned herself to her childless state, which she understood as a condition imposed on her—first by the model of parenting provided by her mother and then by her husband.

Yet, much as Gail wished to rewrite her history to include motherhood, it seemed as though she was in fact living a life that made sense for her in many ways. When she stopped to think about how her life would have been different had she had children, she was not at all sure how welcome those differences would have been. She was deeply invested in her career as a dancer and choreographer, and enjoyed the freedom of being able to study or tour abroad without the sense of guilt she might have experienced had she been leaving a small child behind. She very much enjoyed being taken care of by her very nurturant husband; would she have felt so happy sharing him with a child? She was also terrified of the bodily changes pregnancy brings. As she said, "Getting fat and out of shape is every dancer's worst nightmare!"

I believe that, had Gail received the kind of psychotherapy that connects the present to the past, she might have put all of this together and realized that she had, in fact, chosen not to have children. Her bitterness resulted from her misperception that her childlessness had "just happened" to her.

At the opposite end of the spectrum from Gail was Liza, one of my interviewees most at ease with her nonmaternal existence. "Recently," she told me, "I registered for a class on Women in Islam and I thought, this is great! Not to have to twist my life around in order to pursue my deepest interests. That's one of the loveliest things. It's what makes me feel well adjusted."

It was three years since Liza had surprised herself by clearly, consciously, and without conflict defining herself: she was a woman who did not want to become a mother. As she put it, "The clock just never ticked." She had made the decision when, having recently married at age 37, her gynecologist had threatened her with a "now or never."

"It became very concrete for me; I didn't have a moment's thought about having a kid. And that surprised me. "

At the time, Liza explained her decision to herself in terms of the context of her life. She had married a man who did not want children—but, as he told her, he was ready to go along with any decision she made. An equally important factor was her acting career. Liza was committed to developing her craft by taking on interesting, typically low-paying work. She did not want to feel pressured financially into taking less gratifying, more commercial roles. And she did not want to resent her child for putting her in a position where she might have to. Her husband, too, needed time and space to pursue his academic career.

Looking back at her decision three years later, Liza realized that it had been the right one for her in a far more important way than she had originally perceived.

"Six or seven years ago," Liza told me, "I realized that my mother didn't want to have kids. She never consciously understood that, but I don't think motherhood was really something she wanted. And it's made me think now that that's why I don't want kids, though I'm more conscious of it than my mother was, and maybe I would be a better mother than she was."

Liza described both her mother and her father as "dismal parents—they were like children themselves. They had no idea what nurturing on an emotional or psychological level meant. I feel like I could have lived with strangers who fed and clothed me."

Nevertheless, Liza always felt that she had a choice regarding motherhood; she never felt that either having or not having children was her fate. "I'm very well read and I know one doesn't have to repeat the same mistakes," she said. "I guess I just don't want to make my mother's journey.

"One can be deprived being a parent as well as not being. My mother was deprived by being a parent. You know, I don't think that would necessarily be true for me, but I guess I just didn't want to take the risk." The fact that neither Liza's mother nor her father had ever put any pressure on her to become a mother—had never even broached the subject—was another telling sign that they did not necessarily think parenthood was to be encouraged.

Though she had no children, Lisa felt that she did have a role in helping the next generation by being a mentor to young actors. "This is how I nurture people," she told me.

Liza made sure to keep reminding herself of why she had made her choice. Around her 40th birthday she had experienced a common "turning 40" moment and wondered if it was connected to her childlessness. Maybe, she told herself, she should have a child while she was still able to. But she quickly dismissed the thought.

"I like that I say to myself, 'Maybe you should have a kid,' because it makes me articulate my reasons for not having one. I have a sense of the freedoms lost in becoming a mother. And I think I understand now that whatever choice you make—to have or not to have—there is a sacrifice inherent, and it's a matter of saying, Which sacrifice do I want to make?"

Feeling Incomplete

Women without children often find themselves having to defend against our culture's lingering conception of the childless woman as unhappy, unwomanly, selfish, even dangerous.

Liza was sufficiently sure of her identity as a woman that she was able to shake off the unspoken assumptions of others. "Sometimes," she said, " I look at women with kids who think I'm missing something, and I wonder about them. How can they think they would not be complete without a kid? I feel some women are threatened that I have a sense of completion without being a mother."

Liza felt compelled to counter common notions about women who are not mothers. "One of the things I find myself doing when I talk about not having kids, is saying, 'But I like kids!' I may be doing it because one of society's misconceptions is that women without kids don't like them." Liza had comfortably accepted that, though she really enjoyed children of 8 or 9 and up, she did not have strong feelings about babies or small children.

A woman who does not really understand why she chose not to have children is more vulnerable to negative feelings of "I'm not really a 'good enough' woman"—even though not becoming a mother might make very good, positive sense for her.

Janine, who entered treatment with me in her thirties, felt she needed help because she was convinced that her desire to be childless meant there was something psychologically wrong with her. She thought she was "sick."

She had been married in her twenties and although she worked, she was not particularly happy with or committed to her job; certainly, career was not something that had pulled her away from motherhood. However, she was happy with her life as a married woman. She had met her husband in college. She described him as "the best thing that ever happened to me," a wonderful, caring man. The only tension between her and her husband centered around the issue of children. He was a very nurturant man who wanted kids, and he felt that Janine too would feel happier with her life were she to become a mother.

In treatment Janine's clearest statements, when she was comfortable enough with me, were, "No, I do not want children." We explored her lack of desire for children, and why it made sense for her not to be a mother.

Throughout most of Janine's childhood her mother had been seriously depressed and frequently hospitalized. When she was home, Janine experienced her as distant. Janine's older sister, who was just "nice enough," had provided most of the custodial care during their mother's repeated hospitalizations. Her father, a sanitation worker, had worked extra shifts to ensure a decent living for the family; he was devoted but not particularly available.

As we addressed Janine's occasional but deep depressions, it became clear to her that she was frightened of repeating her depressed mother's history of unavailable parenting. What if she weren't different enough? She felt she could not risk it.

Why was Janine not willing to take that risk, where another woman with an unavailable mother might feel that motherhood *was* worth the risk? Why did Janine not feel it was worth struggling with her anxiety about repeating her mother's mothering while some other women are? Janine was never ambivalent; there was nothing in her experience with kids that intrigued her, gave her pleasure, or made her feel good; she had no pull toward being maternal. And she had no desire for the wide variety of life experiences to which a woman who chooses to mother might look forward. In fact, her only ambivalence about being childless came from her sense of herself as "not right." Our job was to help her understand this.

With psychotherapy to deepen her understanding of herself, Janine began to be more accepting of who she was. Leaving aside the issue of depression, she realized the simple fact that no part of her yearned for a child of her own. She was increasingly able to face the difference between herself and her husband. They worked together, caring enough for each other to be able to reach a creative resolution—he became a successful social worker specializing in child therapy; they stopped discussing the issue of becoming parents; and she came to terms with the fact that her choice had been the right one for her—not sick, not abnormal, but a clear form of, as she came to call it, "self-preservation."

"I Must Be Selfish"

Maggie was 40 at the time I interviewed her and had a 23-year-old daughter. But she was not a mother. She had given birth to her child at age 17 as a single mother, and had lived with her baby in her parents' home for three miserable years. During that time her mother scorned every detail of her mothering. She could do nothing right. This perpetual criticism was a relentlessly harsh echo from Maggie's childhood.

Maggie finally gave up her 3-year-old to be legally adopted by her married cousin, who was infertile, and who Maggie had always seen as a caring older sister. By then Maggie was 20, and knew two things for sure: she did not want her child to grow up in her parents' miserable home, and she did not want to be a mother to any child—not now, not ever.

Maggie's rejection of motherhood was complicated but clear. Having been verbally and physically abused by both her parents while she was growing up, she terrified herself one day when she felt the impulse to hit her infant daughter to stop her from crying. In giving her child up, she hoped to provide her with a good and safe home, while still remaining close to her as an ever-present, adoring "aunt" in her life. And indeed, Maggie has remained a very important person in her daughter's growing up.

Nevertheless, as we spoke, Maggie was filled with guilt over having relinquished her mothering role. "I know that not wanting to be a mother is very selfish," she told me.

"Why do you say that's selfish?"

"That's what my mother told me I was."

"Why do you think she said that?"

"She always says I do everything wrong."

"So, her saying you're selfish is just another way of hurting you, right?"

"What do you mean?"

"What is selfish about giving your child a home and keeping her safe from what might be your impulses to hurt her? I wouldn't call that selfish."

Maggie stopped dead in her tracks. This was a stunning new perception, a revelation. I continued to explain to her that, dedicated as she had been as an "aunt" to her daughter, she had given her up because she really believed that this was what was best for the child.

Many women who choose not to mother a child—whether they never have one or they give up the child they have borne—see themselves as selfish, even if their choice really is in the best interests of the child that is or might have been. It is a reflection of society's most consistent, biased criticism of the childless woman: she is not prepared to give up anything. And the worst thing you can say to any woman is that she is selfish. It feels worse than unwomanly. It feels worse than unfeminine. It cuts to the heart of what a good woman is supposed to be.

A woman who chooses not to become a mother because she fears the inevitable repetition of destructive impulses is far from selfish. Is it self*less* to have a child you don't want? Is it self*less* to have a child to keep you company in your old age? The lines between selfish and selfless become very blurry when we explore women's motives for motherhood.

I believe that it is not selfish to remain childless, even if the choice is made on the basis of your own needs as you perceive them. A woman who feels she has no room in her busy working life for a child, for instance, or who fears that having a child would upset the balance of her marriage, is not being selfish. Is it selfish to want to avoid bringing into the world a child whom you know you might resent? Is it selfish not to want a child because you have never felt any maternal pulls, because you are unmoved by children? Or might it really make good sense?

We can be generous and caring people without being maternal. We can be generative in the sense of creating something that will have a life beyond our own—for example, as artists, teachers, scientists—without being maternal.

In fact, the idea that women who choose not to be mothers are by definition selfish is as mythical as the idea that anyone who mothers is by definition selfless.

So why, in this day and age, do we consider childless women selfish?

It can be a way for those who can't imagine not wanting children to explain the inexplicable lack of such a desire in others. It can be a way for mothers struggling to have and do it all to defend against their own sense of lost freedoms, by scorning the woman who has chosen freedom over motherhood.

I remember a friend of mine telling me how she had asked a group of mothers in a playground whether they considered a woman without children to be "childless" or "childfree." Her question made them furious. They were all struggling to balance work and parenting; they were shredded up trying to feel good about themselves as nurturers while keeping pace in their careers. Any acknowledgment of envy for the childless woman's freedoms had to make them feel terribly guilty, as if they had betrayed their own children. How could they admit to themselves that, though they had gained enormously in becoming parents to the children they surely loved, they had also lost something very dear to them?

Finding a Place in the World

"I come home and make lists of couples who didn't want children," one woman told me. "It makes me realize that I'm not so unique." This woman did not like that "unique" feeling. Other women I interviewed didn't mind it—some rather liked it. It's just a question of personality.

My interviewee's sense of herself as unique—going against the norm—made her feel ashamed of her childlessness. Another woman's uncomfortable feeling of "uniqueness" was alleviated somewhat by the fact that she and her husband had sought out and befriended a number of other childless couples. Women who work in professions that tend to attract "career women" often find it easier to meet other childless women with whom they can identify and who mirror a sense of their choice as okay.

We look to those closest to us for a reflection of ourselves as "good." When our parents, for instance, are pleased with us, we feel that we are loved. Because we are loved, we feel lovable. As we grow we internalize the way we are mirrored. The same is true of the reflection of ourselves we receive from society at large, and from our own community in particular. We want to feel that we belong, that we're acceptable, that we are likable. Otherwise, how can we like ourselves?

That's why it is so important for the woman who is not socially comfortable with her childlessness to find a place in the world where her identity is mirrored, at least to some extent. This might mean letting go of friends who have become parents and actively seeking out people whose lives are not organized around family. It might even mean moving somewhere else.

One woman I know had moved with her husband, soon after their marriage, to a suburban community whose main attraction was safe streets and good schools—perfect for families. When she realized that they would never have children, she began to feel as if she didn't fit. The main point of contact among the people in her neighborhood was around kids—play dates, playgrounds, pediatrician referrals, the PTA. When she met someone new, the first question was always "How many kids do you have?" It was only after she and her husband moved back to the city that she began to feel "normal" again.

ABSENCE AS SPACE

Whichever route a woman chooses, she is likely to experience some sense of loss, especially if she was ambivalent in her choosing. Either way, the feeling of fullness and wholeness she found in her identity and her fantasies of her future self are replaced by an absence. Who is she now? What is her place in the world?

But loss can also be an opportunity for gain.

If a woman without children can accept the parts of herself that held off from motherhood, she is likely to find somewhere within her an attachment to the freedom her life affords her. She can capitalize on enjoying that quality. She can be generative and creative in ways more appropriate to who she is.

If a woman with children can accept the part of herself that was willing to give up a certain kind of freedom, she will focus more on the sense of connectedness that has replaced it.

In her book on childless women, *Reconceiving Women* (1993), psychologist Mardy Ireland offers a wonderful insight into how we can transform the feeling of absence by understanding absence as potential space. By finding a language through which to understand her childlessness, a woman creates a distance between her self as she actually is, and her experience of lacking something. She can then concentrate on creatively filling the space between the two. The vacuum left by her perceived loss is transformed into an opportunity to redirect herself, to find alternate goals, to reinvest her energies. She might find that she can emphasize the activities in her life that are maternal in essence—in the sense of caring for others—or that she can more easily forgo the maternal role and concentrate instead on nonnurturant activities that feel more consonant with her sense of self.

The feminist lesbian poet Irena Klepfisz (1990) has written very candidly about her coming to terms with childlessness. For her, this meant not only dealing with issues of selfishness—although with a different twist—and with being different; it also meant looking carefully at her personal fantasies about motherhood and filling the absence she felt in her life with a different kind of fullness.

Klepfisz describes how, for many years, she lived with a dream of motherhood and a pressing desire to have a child. Still childless at the age of 35, she could scarcely admit to herself or to others that this was to be her destiny. The implications were too devastating.

As the daughter of a Holocaust survivor whose entire family had perished, Klepfisz knew that she was expected to continue the family line. Her mother wanted a grandchild, and the combined voices of the survivors and the lost counted on her to serve both past and future by creating a "normal" family in courageous defiance of her family's devastation.

Not to do so was selfish, sinful.

In any case, not to have a child was very selfish—even without such tragic freight.

Klepfisz accepted this vision of herself as selfish. It was an excuse for not doing what women are supposed to do, particularly her mother's daughter. But how would she ever become the caring, supportive person a woman should be when there was no one to care for? This question troubled her immensely.

Without another person to care for, how would she find a sense of connectedness in her own life? She was haunted by the terrifying image of the bag lady, cut adrift from society by her aloneness, uncared for in her old age, utterly forgotten.

Having a child, she believed, was the only safeguard against such an end; only blood connections endure.

At the age of 36 Klepfisz knew that if she were going to have the child she had yearned for so long, it would have to be soon. She did nothing. By now she had accepted the possibility of loneliness.

But it was mitigated. Bag ladies might be mothers too; where are *their* daughters? She began to recognize her notion that blood connections necessarily endure as a mere fantasy of motherhood.

She also looked inward and discovered that her yearning to care for and support a child of her own was in fact a yearning to care for and support herself. "Thus my desire to become the perfect mother, to act out that fantasy, has in reality nothing to do with having a child, but rather with my desire to experience something I wish I had experienced. It is not a child I wish to mother, it is myself" (Klepfisz 1990, p. 9).

And what of becoming the caring person she longed to be? She had believed that motherhood was the only route for a woman. She had also looked to motherhood as the only way for a woman to have a role in the future. In her evolution she rejected the inevitable fate, the burden of having to become a mother. Her creativity and her generativity became her poetry and her teaching. She has become a guiding force to a generation of lesbian women.

Absence as Space in Motherhood

Women who are mothers can also see as space the absence created by certain kinds of loss: loss of freedoms, loss of professional standing, loss of a certain intimacy with one's partner.

One woman I know, a graduate of Yale Law School, was well on her way to becoming a partner in a prestigious law firm when she became pregnant with her first child. Eve tried to arrange to work part-time so she would not have to interrupt the momentum of her career or lose her sense of herself as a high-powered lawyer who did her job excellently and with relish. She could not imagine anything quite replacing that. But her firm said, "All or nothing." After a great deal of struggle she chose to quit; she knew that in a couple of years she would be able to go back again.

Eve's first year of motherhood was a constant struggle between her enjoyment of her baby and her sense of loss. She would talk to colleagues still in the firm and feel terribly out of touch, terribly envious. She sat in the playground and thought of all the work she could be doing. At the same time she felt she was doing the right thing for herself and her child. She would not have wanted to miss this for anything.

And then when her son was about a year old, Eve became pregnant again. Was she going to have this second child, take off more time from work and risk never being able to go back? She decided she would. And she would make the most of it.

Eve really threw herself into life as a full-time mother-of-two. It was when she got involved in setting up a preschool nursery in her neighborhood that she became conscious of the possibilities for excitement and accomplishment that existed in mothering.

Without having to struggle to have it all, she found she could channel her considerable energies and talents into her job as a mother *and*, by acting as an advocate for neighborhood kids in general, be a part of the world she thought she had lost. She no longer had a title or an office; her desk was cluttered with school correspondence and the occasional baby bottle. But she felt perfectly fulfilled.

Eve's brief moment of glory came when she was invited to help inaugurate a new and desperately needed playground in her community. She had lobbied hard to gain approval and funds for this playground to be built on an empty lot pending development, leading a local task force in the fight.

Both Eve and Klepfisz, in the process of dispelling their personal fantasies and the societal mandates that had made each feel "less than," discovered the capacity to experience absence as space and to creatively fill it. In striking their particular bargains, they both lost something they always thought they would have, but having taken the risk, each gained something she had never expected.

As one woman whom I spoke with said:

"As a mature person I have to be able to say, I might have regrets about this sometimes, about what could have been. But who knows what could have been?"

References

Badinter, E. (1989a). Maternal indifference. In *French Feminist Thought*, ed. T. Moi, pp. 150–177. Oxford: Basil Blackwell.
——— (1989b). *The Unopposite Sex: The End of the Gender Battle*, trans. B. Wright. New York: Harper & Row.

Bateson, M. C. (1989). *Composing a Life*. New York: Atlantic Monthly.

Bernstein, A. E., and Lenhart, S. L., eds. (1993). *The Psychodynamic Treatment of Women*. Washington, DC: American Psychiatric Press.

Carter, J. W., and Carter, M. (1989). *Sweet Grapes: How to Stop Being Infertile and Start Living Again*. Indianapolis: Perspectives Press.

Chodorow, N. J. (1978). *The Reproduction of Mothering: Psychoanalysis and the Sociology of Gender*. Berkeley: University of California Press.

de Beauvoir, S. (1953). *The Second Sex*. New York: Knopf.

Deutsch, H. (1945). *Psychology of Women*, vol. 2. New York: Grune & Stratton.

Duras, M. (1990). The smell of chemicals. In *Practicalities*, pp. 3–5. New York: Grove Weidenfeld.

First, E. (1994). Mothering, hate, and Winnicott. In *Representations of Motherhood*, ed. D. Bassin, M. Honey, and M. M. Kaplan, pp. 147–161. New Haven, CT: Yale University Press.

Friedan, B. (1963). *The Feminine Mystique*. New York: Norton.

Gilligan, C. (1992). *In a Different Voice: Psychological Theory and Women's Development*. Cambridge, MA: Harvard University Press.

Hochschild, A. (1989). *Second Shift: Working Parents and the Revolution at Home*. New York: Viking.

Ireland, M. (1993). *Reconceiving Women: Separating Motherhood from Female Identity*. New York: Guilford.

Klepfisz, I. (1990). Women without children/women without families/women alone. In *Dreams of an Insomniac*, pp. 3–14. Portland, OR: Eighth Mountain Press.

Leach, P. (1994). *Children First: What Our Society Must Do*. New York: Knopf.

Maloney, J. (1993). A perfect right to love. *The Sun* 215:20–23, November. Chapel Hill, NC.

Mead, M. (1972). *Blackberry Winter: My Earlier Years*. New York: Simon & Schuster.

Miller, J. B. (1976). *Toward a New Psychology of Women*. Boston: Beacon.

Rich, A. (1976). *Of Woman Born: Motherhood as Experience and Institution*. New York: Norton.

Rosenblatt, J. S. (1970). Views on the onset and maintenance of maternal behavior in the rat. In *Development and Evolution of Behavior: Essays in Honor of T. C. Schneirla*, ed. L. R. Aronson, E. Tobach, D. S. Lehrman, and J. S. Rosenblatt, pp. 489–515. San Francisco: Freeman.

Schwartz, A. (1994). Taking the nature out of mother. In *Representations of Motherhood*, ed. D. Bassin, M. Honey, and M. M. Kaplan, pp. 240–255. New Haven, CT: Yale University Press.

Schwartz, J. D. (1993). *The Mother Puzzle: A New Generation Reckons with Motherhood*. New York: Simon & Schuster.

Tannen, D. (1992). The real Hillary factor. *The New York Times*, October 12, Op-Ed. p. A19.

Winnicott, D. W. (1955). *The Maturational Processes and the Facilitating Environment*. New York: International Universities Press.

Ziman-Tobin, P. O. (1986). Childless women at midlife. In *The Psychology of Today's Woman: New Psychoanalytic Visions*, ed. T. Bernay and D. W. Cantor, pp. 305–317. Hillsdale, NJ: Analytic Press.

Further Reading

Bair, D. (1990). *Simone de Beauvoir: A Biography*. New York: Summit.

Butler, J. (1993). *Bodies that Matter*. London: Routledge.

Chodorow, N. J. (1984). *Femininities, Masculinities, Sexualities: Freud and Beyond*. Lexington, KY: University Press of Kentucky.

Debold, E., Wilson, M., and Malave, I. (1993). *Mother Daughter Revolution: From Betrayal to Power*. Reading, MA: Addison Wesley.

Dowrick, S., and Grundberg, S., eds. (1980). *Why Children?* New York: Harcourt Brace Jovanovich.

Ehrenreich, B., and English, D. (1978). *For Her Own Good: 150 Years of the Experts' Advice to Women*. New York: Anchor/Doubleday.

Eisenstein, H. (1983). *Contemporary Feminist Thought*. Boston: Hall.

Eyer, D. (1992). *Mother–Infant Bonding: A Scientific Fiction*. New Haven, CT: Yale University Press.

Fabe, M., and Wikler, N. (1979). *Up against the Clock: Career Women Speak on the Choice to Have Children*. New York: Warner.

Fausto-Sterling, A. (1985). *Myths of Gender: Biological Theories about Women and Men*. New York: Basic Books.

Felman, S. (1993). *What Does a Woman Want? Reading and Sexual Difference*. Baltimore: Johns Hopkins University Press.

Fleming, A. T. (1994). *Motherhood Deferred: A Woman's Journey*. New York: Fawcett Columbine.

Freud, S. (1925). Some psychological consequences of the anatomical distinction between the sexes. *Standard Edition* 19:248–258.

—— (1931). Female sexuality. *Standard Edition* 21:225–243.

Gerson, K. (1985). *Hard Choices: How Women Decide about Work, Career, and Motherhood.* Berkeley: University of California Press.

Gerson, M.-J., Posner, J.-A., and Morros, A. M. (1991). The wish for a child in couples eager, disinterested, and conflicted about having children. *American Journal of Family Therapy* 19(4):334–343.

Glenn, E. N., Chang, G., and Forcey, L. R., eds. (1994). *Mothering: Ideology, Experience, and Agency.* London: Routledge.

Glickman, R. L. (1993). *Daughters of Feminists.* New York: St. Martin's Press.

Hays, S. (1996). *The Cultural Contradictions of Motherhood.* New Haven, CT: Yale University Press.

Hubbard, R. (1990). *The Politics of Women's Biology.* New Brunswick, NJ: Rutgers University Press.

Lang, S. S. (1991). *Women without Children.* New York: Pharos.

Lewontin, R. C., Rose, S., and Kamin, L. J. (1984). *Not In Our Genes: Biology, Ideology, and Human Nature.* New York: Pantheon.

Lorber, J. (1994). *Paradoxes of Gender.* New Haven, CT: Yale University Press.

Margolis, F. R. (1987). *Women and achievement: the role of sex stereotypes in theory, reality and psychic structure.* Unpublished Ph.D. dissertation, City University of New York.

Marshall, M. M. (1993). *Good Enough Mothers.* Princeton, NJ: Peterson's.

Mattes, J. (1994). *Single Mothers by Choice.* New York: Times Books.

Money, J., and Ehrhardt, A. (1972). *Man and Woman, Boy and Girl: The Differentiation and Dimorphism of Gender Identity from Conception to Maturity*. Baltimore: Johns Hopkins University Press.

Notman, M. T., and Nadelson, C. C., eds. (1991). *Men and Women: New Perspectives on Gender Differences*. Washington, DC: American Psychiatric Press.

Pies, C. (1988). *Considering Parenthood*. San Francisco: Spinsters/ Aunt Lute.

Robertson, J. A. (1994). *Children of Choice: Freedom and the New Reproductive Technologies*. Princeton, NJ: Princeton University Press.

Rosaldo, M. Z., and Lampere, L., eds. (1974). *Women, Culture and Society*. Stanford, CA: Stanford University Press.

Salzer, L. P. (1991). *Surviving Infertility: A Compassionate Guide through the Emotional Crisis of Infertility*. New York: Harper Perennial.

Shalev, C. (1989). *Birth Power*. New Haven, CT: Yale University Press.

Sheehy, G. (1991). *The Silent Passage: Menopause*. New York: Random House.

Stoller, R. J. (1985). *Presentations of Gender*. New Haven, CT: Yale University Press.

Stotland, N. L., ed. (1990). *Psychiatric Aspects of Reproductive Technology*. Washington, DC: American Psychiatric Press.

Thurer, S. (1994). *The Myths of Motherhood: How Culture Reinvents the Good Mother*. Boston: Houghton Mifflin.

Veevers, J. E. (1980). *Childless by Choice*. Toronto: Butterworth.

Index